A COMPASS TO PARENTING

A COMPASS TO PARENTING

Eleven Essential Ways to Nurture, Love, and Instruct Your Child

LYDIA WEATHERLY

iUniverse, Inc.
Bloomington

A Compass to Parenting
Eleven Essential Ways to Nurture, Love, and Instruct Your Child

iUniverse books may be ordered through booksellers or by contacting:

iUniverse
1663 Liberty Drive
Bloomington, IN 47403
www.iuniverse.com
1-800-Authors (1-800-288-4677)

ISBN: 978-1-4697-5355-3 (sc)
ISBN: 978-1-4697-5356-0 (e)
ISBN: 978-1-4697-5357-7 (dj)

Printed in the United States of America

iUniverse rev. date: 3/9/2012

Contents

Part One
The Starting Point:

Setting Your Course
The Power of Influence
Parenting with Purpose

Introduction
Setting Your Course

If there is anything that we wish to change in the child, we should first examine it and see whether it is not something that could better be changed in ourselves.

—*C. G. Jung*

On occasion, our immediate family would go to Coeur D'Alene Lake in Idaho for the Fourth of July fireworks display. One time we took our wakeboarding boat to join some friends on their larger boat. The kids wanted to do some wakeboarding while we were hanging out on our friends' boat, so we tied our boat to the larger boat so they could wakeboard at any time. We spent the day on the lake and enjoyed watching the fireworks that evening.

A lot of people go to Coeur D'Alene Lake for the Fourth of July celebration—it is a beautiful backdrop for fireworks—so navigating through the traffic after the fireworks is intense, and traffic jams are a promised part of it. We pulled our boat out of the water and headed home to Spokane, Washington. Obviously, we anticipated a long wait at numerous traffic lights and that the freeway would be slow moving. My husband set out to beat the system and find his own way home (this was before we had a navigation system in our car, so he relied on his memory to direct him). His plan started out very promising;

it was a beautiful drive up and around a mountain road that would take us near Spokane, where we then could jump onto the freeway to get us home.

About forty minutes into the trip, we came to a T in the road. My husband, who has an incredible built-in road map in his brain, stopped at the T and carefully deliberated whether to turn right or left. The kids in the back were emphatically telling him to turn right but alas, he went left. About twenty minutes later, we ended up back at the same T in the road!

If it had not been dark, I would have seen my husband's face turn red. We all laughed, but in his children's eyes, his directional reputation has not been the same since that day. In my husband's defense, though, the twenty-minute cruise through the mountains did allow the traffic on the freeway to dissipate.

You might have a navigation system in your car. Having such a "compass" in your car saves you time and frustration and brings security and peace, because you have something that will aid you in finding your way to your destination. I love the navigation system in our current car, because even if I make a wrong turn, I can turn it on and punch in the address, and it will redirect me to my destination.

Having a sophisticated navigation system can be a time-saver, but even a simple compass enables you to find your way back to where you want to be when you get lost or confused. The same thing can happen in parenting: we can get lost in the duties, routines, agendas, chaos, problems, and confusion in our parenting role. If we could have our own compass or a road map, then we could look again at the big picture of our role as parents and be redirected when our emotions or energy become drained or overwhelmed.

When we see our destination in parenting and the necessary maneuvers we need to make to reach that destination, we will experience the strength of peace that will move us forward, instead of getting caught up in emotions that may cause us to overanalyze things or to paralyze, exasperate, and defeat us—or worse, make us passive and counterproductive in our attempts to parent effectively. Parenting is full of joy, fond memories, and fun. But we also know it is filled with frustration, fatigue, and failure at times. We need encouragement—the type of encouragement that gives us strength and enthusiasm to go on; the type that says, "You are on the right path. You're really going the right way. Just continue to do what you are doing and in the end, it will all turn out well."

I have been parenting for twenty-nine years. My children are all grown and some are beginning their own families, but I am still learning in my new role: as a parent of adult children and, mixed with that, my role as a grandparent. I have learned a lot from my ignorance and failures in parenting. I have gleaned information from reading many parenting and counseling books about relationships. I really believe if you focus on building strong relationships with your children, it will help diminish the mistakes and failures you will make in parenting your children.

I have taken parenting classes, been trained as a lay counselor, and have served in a counseling ministry at church, all of which have helped me understand myself and my children better. Those educational venues are great, but I believe that experience mixed with knowledge is the best venue of all. This is one reason why I have written this book: to share with you some of that knowledge that comes from a long journey of learning to parent in a way that transforms the characters of both parent and child.

The other reason I have chosen to write this book is that I have a compassionate heart for parents who sincerely are trying their best but are finding parenting exhausting and, at times, disheartening. I want to give you encouragement and passion in the purpose of your parenting. I want to help you see the bigger picture of your purpose in life. I want to ease your anxiety, to show you that this parenting thing is more about you than your child. God has a purpose in your life; he has a goal in mind for you. It is up to you to pursue him and find out what he wants to do in you and through you, within the parameters of parenting.

The eleven ways that we will walk through together in this book are things that I came to realize after parenting my children. Some, I understood and put into practice; others, I learned much later in the parenting years. I truly believe it is critical to focus on and comprehend these eleven things. They will help you center on the most important things. As parents, we tend to "major in the minors" when we raise our children. We know we shouldn't always do that, but we just don't know any better. I believe if you focus on these eleven things in your relationship with your child, you will become a person who is closer to God and become a person of great godly influence in your child's life.

To help you get as much out of this book as possible, I have included study questions for each chapter. These questions will ask you to dig deeper into the things I discuss and ask you to look in the Bible for more help. You can use these questions individually or in a group setting. I am a firm believer in Bible study groups and book study groups. They provide a venue for others to minister to you. I love to have fellow sojourners share my struggles with me. It always brings encouragement and inspiration to my life. I think you will find the same benefit.

God really does have a unique plan for your family and the way you are to parent each child. God has carefully chosen you to come alongside him to fulfill his work. I can see his plan in many situations within the raising of my family as well. Besides giving us three biological children, I can see how God purposely placed additional children in our family at different times. I thought that raising my own three children was more than enough for me to handle, but God had more responsibility and blessings to give us by allowing us to dedicate time to four more children. These additional children came to us at different times, in different ways, and for different reasons. It gave us many opportunities to make even more parenting mistakes but also gave us opportunities to bless them and receive blessings back.

The four foster children are wonderful adults now, making a difference in their spheres of influence. One of the four decided to "adopt" us as his parents, so we have been a very close and intricate part of this man's life for the past thirteen years. Our three biological children and our foster son are believers; we are a close-knit family who enjoys spending time together. Our family is expanding with in-laws; they are grafted into our hearts as our own sons and daughters and treated as such. Of course, there are now grandchildren, who do not take much work at all on the grandparents' part. Well, at least at this time in our lives, we are just here to love them beyond comprehension.

Christian parents want a surefire way to raise children to become Christians. I am here to tell you that no such parenting plan will produce a guaranteed product. There is, however, a commanded role you have from God—to be a significant person in your child's life; a person who will develop a relationship like no other with him/her; a person who will be a representation of God's relationship with us, as much as humanly possible. If you find yourself lost in the parenting role and feel it might be time to move in a different direction, I would suggest you read the following chapters and allow God to mold, shape, challenge, and change you into the unique and sanctified parent he has designed you to be.

I pray that God will use this material to heighten your awareness of how greatly he can use you to impact the world around you and develop an abundance of relationships that are eternal and momentous.

1
The Power of Influence

For I am mindful of the sincere faith within you, which first dwelt in your grandmother Lois, and your mother Eunice, and I am sure that it is in you as well.
2 Timothy 1:5
(New American Standard)

Don't worry that children never listen to you; worry that they are always watching you.

—Robert Fulghum

The power of influence is, strangely, an indirect effort. Most of the time, you don't set out purposely to influence someone. Instead, you usually influence someone by just being you. This indirect effort still has powerful impact but not equal to the effort you put into it. How you live your life will influence those around you. You probably are not fully aware of the power you have and can use to change or affect another person's life. The people around you observe and notice your behavior and attitude. If they spend a considerable amount of time with you, you will have a subtle yet penetrating effect on that person. Now, the question is: what kind of influence do you have on your children? What message are you giving them about who you are, what you stand for, and what is important to you?

Every day, your life reveals a story about you. What you say and do every day reveals something about your past, something about you today, and something about your future hopes, dreams, and desires. Have you thought about what you want to see in your child's life? What in your life do you want to influence them? I want my life to influence my children to live for Christ, not for themselves; for them to make relationships a priority in their lives. I want them to live beyond their fears or insecurities to become the person God has designed them to be. When the last chapter of your life is ending here on earth, when all is "said and done," what do you hope will be written on their hearts through the influence you had on each of their lives?

Parenting Is an Influential Profession

Truly influential people are people who attract others to follow them; others like to be around them. Influential people usually make things happen, whether it is something monumental or minuscule. They make things happen without manipulating, forcing, or controlling.

To be influential, you first need to understand and believe you have an impact on others. You need to realize that people like to be around people who show a genuine interest in them. To be influential you need to

- be friendly;
- be complimentary;
- be a good listener;
- be apologetic, sympathetic, and respectful;
- complain and criticize less;
- not condemn or shame;
- use succinct and amiable words; and
- use a gentle and nonthreatening tone.

Influential people show sincerity and passion about life. They are not big complainers or criticizers. They have opinions and desires, but they don't shame, embarrass, condemn, or belittle yours. They listen to your opinions, convictions, and desires and then gently persuade you to listen to theirs. They move you toward the vision in their mind through their words and, above all, how they share those words. A dictator or manipulator can mislead you because he initially seems like this type of sincere, influential person but will turn into a manipulative person once he has hooked you into following him.

As a believer in Christ, with his power in you, you have the ability to allow Christ's influence to impact those around you. Surrendering and allowing his Spirit to work through you is a deliberate awareness on your part. In the fifth chapter of Galatians, Paul talks about denying the desires of the flesh, refusing to walk in those fleshly (worldly) desires, and following the Spirit's lead. *"But I say, walk by the Spirit, and you will not carry out the desire of the flesh. For the flesh sets its desire against the Spirit, and the Spirit against the flesh; for these are in opposition to one another, so that you may not do the things that you please"* (Galatians 5:16–17, NAS).

In Galatians 5:19–23, we see counterparts to the choices we can make in our life that will produce good or evil in us, which will eventually impact those around us.

Deeds of the Flesh	Deeds of the Spirit
❖ *Immorality*	❖ *Self-control*
❖ *Idolatry*	❖ *Faithfulness*
❖ *Anger*	❖ *Love*
❖ *Dissension*	❖ *Peace*
❖ *Drunkenness*	❖ *Joy*
❖ *Jealousy*	❖ *Kindness*
❖ *Disputes*	❖ *Gentleness*

To walk in the Spirit means to surrender your thoughts and intentions to his thoughts and intentions for your life. To walk in the Spirit means to know and believe that God is in you to will and direct each step you take. Do you want that? If you do, then pursue him.

Live out your day in conscious pursuit of fulfilling his work for you within the parameters of your sphere of influence.

Each of our personal worlds is different from others. Some people have a world that has many, many people and places in it. Others have a smaller world. It doesn't matter how big or small your world is; what is important is that you believe this is the world upon which God has asked you to be an influence. This sphere of influence is your opportunity to make a difference—to be his voice, his hands, and his feet.

You can do that only if you allow him to shine through you and if you allow him to control you. This is a purpose of the Holy Spirit—to glorify God and to put his character on display through your daily life. Are you willing to release your life, to lay it down and replace it with true worship? What is true worship? Worship is bowing before him with a heart that is desirous to praise his worthiness, to be thankful for what he has done for you and for who he is. Worship is sacrificing your viewpoint, desire, goals, and plans in exchange for his viewpoint, desire, goal, and plan for your life. Seek and you shall find; knock and the door will be opened ... to a life that will be filled with significance and purpose.

Parenting is an influential profession. Christian parents have Christ as their compass point to direct and guide them as a changing instrument in the life of their child.

The Power of Influence
(Supplementary questions for personal or group discussion)

1. During your childhood, who was the most influential person you remember?
   - In what way did he/she influence you?
   - How did this influence benefit your adulthood or adversely affect it?
2. What type of influence do you think you personally have on your children? Your spouse? Your friends?
3. What do you want your life to produce in your child?
4. From Galatians 5:13–25, make a list of the flesh's influence and the Spirit's influence. From your list, which influences are you allowing to reign right now?
   - If you have allowed a fleshy characteristic to reign, what characteristic of the Spirit could replace it? (Choose a characteristic quality from your list of the Spirit's influence.)
5. Briefly describe your sphere of influence. Who are the main characters in your world?
   - What role do you have in each of these people lives?
6. From the eight qualities of an influential person, which quality or qualities do you need to improve?

2
Parenting with Purpose

And walking by the Sea of Galilee, He saw two brothers, Simon who was called Peter and Andrew his brother, casting a net into the sea; for they were fishermen. And He said to them, "Follow Me, and I will make you fishers of men." And they immediately left the nets, and followed Him.
Matthew 4:18–20
(NAS)

Before I got married, I had six theories about bringing up children. Now, I have six children and no theories.
—John Wilmot, Earl of Rochester

If I were to ask you what your goal is in parenting, what would you say? Would you say obedient children? Would your answer be that you want to make sure your children are safe, secure, and fed? Maybe your goal is to just love them and teach them to love others. Or perhaps you don't have a particular goal in mind. You might figure, "I'm too busy to think about what my goal is when all I do all day is try to keep everything from getting out of control!" Isn't it amazing how quickly a day passes right by us, because we are knee-deep in managing all the planned and unplanned events of the day? Then, at the end of the day, we ask ourselves, "What in the world did I accomplish today?" You might ask yourself, "Was it meaningful? Did it count for anything?"

Life makes more sense when there is purpose, doesn't it? Purpose is the fuel that propels us forward in any given situation. If you lose your focus on the purpose, you start to sputter, you stall, and you lose the momentum to continue, especially when there is one of those "big hills" to overcome. There has to be a big-picture purpose in your parenting. If you don't have a purpose, how do you know where you're going and how you're going to get there? Having purpose is all about having a goal, about having a destination in mind. It is taking large and small steps to meet that goal or destination.

Changing Our Parenting Philosophy

When I think about the purpose and process of parenting, I think about Matthew 4:18–20. This passage is about two fishermen who are about to take the lessons learned from being fishermen and use them in a new direction: *"And walking by the Sea of Galilee, he saw two brothers, Simon who was called Peter, and Andrew his brother, casting a net into the sea; for they were fishermen. And He said to them, 'Follow Me, and I will make you fishers of men.' And they immediately left their nets and followed Him."*

Being a fisherman is more difficult than we sometimes realize. Being a fisherman requires a lot of energy and stamina. I'm not talking about casual fishing for sport—standing at the end of a dock, hanging your pole out there to see if a perch will nibble on the worm dangling off your hook. What I'm talking about is fishing as a vocation, similar to what you see on the Discovery Channel television show *Deadliest Catch*. This is hard work. There is much to do to prepare to catch fish. You have to take care of your nets and know where and when to maneuver them into place, as well as pulling the nets in at precisely the right time. You need patience to wait for your catch. You need to have courage to tackle any problems or storms that attempt to destroy your efforts. It takes a lot of diligence, wisdom, and hard work to produce a good catch.

Now, let's get back to the story of the men who were fishing. They were busy casting their net into the Sea of Galilee when Jesus arrived on the scene to invite them to follow him and learn to be "fishers of men" instead of fishermen. They immediately responded to the invitation, leaving their nets (which meant leaving what they knew and believed in) to cleave to Jesus, believing and trusting that he would teach and direct them into a life that was purposeful and fulfilling.

The dedication and disposition of a fisherman is similar to the qualities needed to parent effectively and produce the results you desire: it requires stamina, energy, and endurance. You need a plan, a purpose, and a goal. You need to learn timing and patience. It calls for courage, wisdom, and diligence. Parenting is one of the most difficult jobs (and relationships) you will have. To parent actively and productively means you need to be fully engaged in your role as a parent, rather than just focusing on the basic care and protection of your child.

What Jesus was saying to Peter and Andrew was that he would teach them to "catch" men by teaching and persuading them to trust and believe in him, in God. That is how we want to think about ourselves in our roles as parents—we are "fishers of men." Our goal in parenting should be evangelism and then discipleship. In other words, catch them and then direct them.

The Way of a Disciple

How do we evangelize our children? The same way we evangelize others: by being a reflection and a representation of God to them. We are called to be witnesses, to be the light of the world and the salt of the earth. We are called to be image-bearers. We are called to tell our children the gospel of Christ, of how holy God is, and why we need a savior to save us from our sinful selves. We need to show them what it means to repent and be transformed into God's likeness. As we demonstrate our transformation, our children will follow our actions and attitudes. This is what discipleship looks like. It is us, living out our life as a new person (a Christian), and our children following suit. We cannot save them, but we need to show them what true redemption looks like. Romans 12:9–21 has a good checklist for us to evaluate how we look as a Christian. We should

- ❖ *be kind;*
- ❖ *honor one another;*
- ❖ *be enthusiastic and passionate about God;*
- ❖ *serve God and people;*
- ❖ *rejoice;*
- ❖ *be patient;*
- ❖ *be steadfast in prayer; and*
- ❖ *be hospitable.*

In John 15:5, Jesus says, *"I am the vine, you are the branches; he who abides in* [follows] *Me, and I in him, he bears much fruit; for apart from Me you can do nothing."* We cannot be transformed into Jesus's character without abiding in him and allowing him to abide in us. This means surrendering to the Holy Spirit's control. We will look at some character qualities of God that are essential in parenting in the next few chapters, but for now, let's continue focusing on the ultimate purpose of a Christian parent.

Mirror, Mirror, on the Wall …

"You are the light of the world. A city set on a hill cannot be hidden. Nor do people light a lamp and put it under a basket, but on a stand, and it gives light to all in the house. In the same way, let your light shine before others" (Matthew 5:14–16, English Standard Version).

In this passage, Jesus was all about bringing that "light" into the pathway of everyone he encountered (John 8:12, NAS). If our goal in parenting is evangelism and discipleship, then the way we live our lives in our homes should give off the light of Christ to our children. The reflection of Christ in us and our good deeds need to be visible to others; our light should shine bright, shining on all who cross our paths. Our children should be illuminated by the light that shines from within us. There is a "law of reflection" in our world. If you have a mirror and you shine a light into it, it will reflect that light outward. What shines on that mirror will shine out on something else. When we choose to focus our attention on the character qualities of God and allow him to replace our character flaws with his character virtues, it will reflect down to our child.

However, we can lose the value and effectiveness of being transformed into the likeness of Christ (2 Cor. 3:18) if we don't allow his light to shine outward. We darken his light in us by our selfish and sinful attitudes and behaviors. We allow fear or shame to cover his light before men. Our attitudes and actions will display either us or God. We want our children to see God and praise his goodness. A good question to ask yourself daily is "Is my child seeing Jesus in this attitude or action, or is he seeing me in this attitude or action?" I think such a self-evaluating question, at times, would stop us in our tracks. We want our children to be attracted to Christ, like a moth is drawn to a light. We want them to see Christ in us.

Jesus brought light onto the path of those he encountered. It is our responsibility and blessing to *"proclaim the excellencies of Him who has called us out of darkness into His marvelous light"* (1 Peter 2:9, NAS), even though they may not want it or are not aware they are in the dark. We are to illuminate Christ to the world. *"'Let your light shine before men in such a way that they may see your good works, and glorify your Father who is in heaven'"* (Matthew 5:16, NAS).

We are also *"the salt of the earth"* (Matthew 5:13, NAS). We are the preservatives that keep Christ's presence known in this rather dark and depraved world. We are flavor enhancers: we have the opportunity to let our children see how beautiful and good God is. How we live life through Christ's indwelling Spirit can increase and intensify our children's desire to know God personally. Salt blocks provide nutrients for animals but also create a thirst in them. The salt in us should create a thirst for Christ in others. Do you think your child is becoming thirsty for Christ because he can see Jesus in you?

This word salt also was used in scripture to indicate how we are to live in harmony and peace with one another (Mark 9:50; Colossians 4:6). This act of maintaining peaceful relationships in a world full of conflict is a witnessing tool in itself. When Christians live in harmony with one another, it draws attention and questions from the world. How harmonious our homes are will show our children how different Christians are from the world.

These passages indicate we can lose our saltiness, that our salt can become tasteless. If we don't follow Jesus with a wholehearted devotion, we can lose that saltiness. This can happen by compromising God's commands, principles, and truths in our life choices. Saltiness can be lost if it is mixed with other things, such as the world's influences and principles. It is easy for us to compromise obedience to God's Word in order to be more comfortable and acceptable in the world. It is also easy to take God's laws and principles to an extreme, thus becoming legalistic. Such strict conformity to God's laws is a surefire way to dull the saltiness in a Christian.

So, how much of God does your child see when she/he looks at you and listens to you? Have you dimmed your light, or lost some of that saltiness God talks about? If you think you have may I ask you some questions that will help you reflect Christ more. First, how is your relationship with God? Do you spend time talking with him? Second, are you reading your Bible on a regular basis? Are you listening to him? Third, are you being obedient to what you read in the Bible? Are you taking action on what he is telling you to do? The reason I have asked these three questions are because the more we read God's Word, then the more we become aware of our wrong thoughts words, and actions, then the more we allow him to change us into his likeness. This all happens from the inside out. Being a Christian is not behaving like one; it is becoming one. We not only "put on Christ" (Rom. 13:14); but we also "abide in Christ" (Jn 15:4).

A Beautiful Reflection

We forget our children are watching us, sometimes more than we are watching them! The same is true of nonbelievers: they watch us to see if we walk the talk. Does the nonbeliever in your life really see Christ in you? For example, there is a tendency for Christian parents to point out the wrong, or sin, in another person in order to teach their child a lesson or two on what not to say or how not to act. This tactic works well at times, but I think we forget the overall message we might be giving our children in the process: be critical and judgmental of other people. Personally, that is not my intent, so I guess my job is to make sure whatever I say in that situation needs to include compassion, love, and understanding toward the person I am pointing out to my child. For example, "The way that Mary is speaking to her mom is very rude and unloving. I wonder if Mary knows she sounds rude and that she is hurting her mother's feelings. Mary's mom will probably show her how to speak more with love." If I add my care and concern for that person, then my child will pick up on the teaching moment as well as on the compassion and understanding I have for sin in people's lives.

Our children should see our dependency on God and the reason we choose to depend on him. God is trustworthy because he is good, and everything he does is good. His goodness is everything that is meaningful and powerful about his character. God's Word declares he is a good Father. "*O give thanks to the Lord, for He is good; For His loving kindness is everlasting*" (1 Chronicles 16:34, NAS). The word "good" in Hebrew refers to his character, which is pleasant, beautiful, excellent, delightful, joyful, kind, correct, and righteous (2 Chronicles 5:13, 7:3; Ezra 3:11; Psalms 106:1, 136:1; Jeremiah 33:11). As Psalm 119:68 tells us, God is good, and he does good. God's intention is to *be* good, to *be* pleasant, to *be* beautiful, to *be* excellent, to *be* delightful, to *be* joyful, and to *be* correct, kind, and righteous to his children. He is intent on putting his goodness on display through his actions. What a beautifully "good" description of who God is—he is good. He is all that defines good.

If I see God as having these wonderful attributes, that vision will produce a desire to enjoy that part of him, and it will produce a desire in me to give it out to others. Do you want your children to see God like this? Revealing God's goodness to your children is like building a house for them, in which they can find security and peace. His love, grace, mercy, patience, wisdom, and forgiveness all supply what is needed for his children to know they are safe and secure in his house. Through the difficulties of life, we want our children not only to come to us to find encouragement and strength, but we also want them to ultimately go to their Father in heaven to find the kind of encouragement and strength only he can give. He is their ultimate compass in life; we are just instruments pointing the way.

Walking the life of faith is not safe. It can be painful, unstable, and trying at times. Showing your children that you confidently put your trust in God's wisdom, will, and power in your life will give your children the confidence to put their trust in him someday.

Parenting with Purpose

(Supplementary questions for personal or group discussion)

1. Write out a mission statement that includes your purpose in parenting. *Example: My purpose in parenting my child is to show her the love of Christ through my daily interactions with her.*
2. What steps must you take to fulfill your purpose in parenting?
3. Do you verbally share with your child how good God is?
   - In what circumstances can you share about the goodness of God with your child?
4. In what circumstance are you having difficulty seeing God's goodness right now?
   - What scriptural truth can you apply that will help you believe that God's goodness is stamped all over the circumstance? Write it out.
5. What memory stands out to you when you haven't been the "light" or "salt" of Christ to a nonbeliever, to your child, or to another Christian?
6. What would you have done differently to be more of the "light" or "salt" of Christ?
7. Answer the questions that are listed in the last paragraph under the heading "Mirror, Mirror, on the Wall …"

Part Two
Three Essential Character
Qualities in Parenting:

Love
Grace
Patience

3
The Quality of Love

But God demonstrates His own love toward us, in that while we were
yet sinners, Christ died for us.
Romans 5:8
(NAS)

The love of God is like the ocean: you can see its beginnings
but not its end.

—Anonymous

My mind is camped on the song "Jesus Loves Me." I have heard that song in Sunday school, vacation Bible school, and sometimes even in a church worship service. I would guess that you, too, have sung that song to your little one at some time. As parents, we continually tell our children that God loves them. Our heart's desire is to have them experience Christ's love in their own hearts. We try to convey this truth to them—that God actually does love them personally. But there could be one huge barrier to convincing your children that Jesus loves them: your own belief and understanding of God's love for you. It has been said that you can only impart what you possess. Do you really believe God loves you? Do you feel God's love within the difficult circumstance you may be in right now, the situation that you know God could eliminate if he chose to? You may ask yourself at times, "Is he really a loving God?"

Two Brands of Love

If someone were to ask you to define God's love, what would you say? I would say that there is only one true way to define what his love looks like, and that is through his written word. We see his love described in such passages as 1 John 4:7–21, where we see that the essence, the core of God, is love. We see the different shades of love in John 21:15–18, where Christ defines the difference between "agapao" and "phileo" love. *Agapao* love is a deep, sacrificial type of love; *phileo* is a close-friendship type of love. In Ephesians 5:22–28, there is the beautiful analogy of the bride and bridegroom's love relationship, which is a picture of Christ's love for his church.

After you read such passages as these, you begin to realize that *God defines his love by his relationships*—the relationship he has with his Son, with his people, and even with those who reject him. His love is displayed as pure, wholesome, and untainted. Have you noticed that God's love always guides his relationship with us? Because he loves me, he directs me to spend time with him through prayer and spending time reading the Bible. He makes certain things happen in my life that will grow me closer to him and will change an attitude that is not pleasing to him, nor profitable for me. He always challenges me to be more like him. Why? Because he loves me and wants my life to be full of joy … to be full of him.

Would you say it is easier to describe the love the world has created than it is to describe God's love? I would. The love the world has created seems a bit more tangible. If I understand and experience God's love, I will be less likely to adopt the type of love the world displays. *Webster's Dictionary* has a good grip on the definition of the world's brand of love. According to *Webster's*, love means "to feel an affection for, to be in love with, to be fond of, to be attracted to, passionate attraction and desire towards, romantic affair,"[1] and so on. Although some of these definitions are true to God's definition of love, the way they are portrayed and carried out in the world looks a bit different from what our Lord intended love to look like. Hollywood, romance novels, television, and trendy magazines all give us the view that love is physical, conditional, temporary, transitional, and easily discarded. We must make sure the love that resides in our hearts is not clouded or polluted with the love the world defines and displays.

Believing God Loves Me

To understand someone, you need to spend time with that person. You listen and seek out the entirety of that person. That is why defining God's love is essential to our understanding of his way of loving. Once we understand how he describes love in scripture, it is easier for us to actually believe he does love us. It is easier to recognize when he is showing his love to us. This is where we can fail as Christian parents—by not personally believing that God loves us deeply, completely, and unconditionally. Can we compellingly teach our children that God loves them when we are doubting it ourselves? We can only testify to something we truly believe.

So let's face our doubts and ponder God's love for us. First, God never declared his love for us without demonstrating it first. Creation was God's first action of his love for us—he had to love us in order to want to create us. What a beautiful thought! It is similar to our desire to have a child. We want to give our love to our own creation, in a sense. We want to raise a child up in the image of ourselves (hopefully, with many improvements!). We want to take care of that child, physically and spiritually. We want to train the child so she will become a valued member of society, in the hope she will one day make a difference in this world. We want to do all this for our children because we love them.

Second, because God is love, what else would pour out of him as he created us? In John 5:20, it says, *"God loves the Son and shows him all things that he himself is doing,"* and John 17:24 states that God loved Jesus *"before the foundation of the world."* John 14:31 declares that Christ loves the Father. God fathered his children, Israel, throughout their journeys with him. He took care of every spiritual and physical need. God always came through for them as they suffered affliction, so we see love began with God and love comes from God. Third, love came down as the ultimate love act for mankind—the gift of salvation through the redemptive blood of Christ. God's love for us is priceless. These are all demonstrations of God's love for mankind. *God validates his love for us through his actions.*

The Measure of Our Love

The second greatest commandment is *"You shall love your neighbor as yourself"* (Mark 12:31, NAS). God calls us to put human hands and feet onto his holy love. It is not surprising that God insisted on our loving him first and then loving others—these are the two most important commandments. It is not surprising, because he knows we need to experience and embrace his love before we can love others sacrificially. By nature, we are very selfish. We tend to seek out what is best for us in a relationship. God's love is not always based on an emotional feeling. His love is a decision he has made to love us, regardless of our response or behavior. The more we cultivate our love relationship with God, the more our love for others will increase.

Do we really love God with all our being? Do we really love each other by God's standard or definition? This supernatural love he calls us to display is the biggest witnessing tool he has given us. Matthew 5:16 says, *"Let your light shine before men in such a way that they may see your good works, and glorify your Father who is in heaven."* People will be drawn to give God praise, esteem, and recognition through you; your good work is Christ working through you. Displaying his love to our children is witnessing to them the greatness of God's love for them personally. We need to be attentive in evaluating the kind of love we portray to our children. Are we loving selfishly or sacrificially? How we love our children will give them reason to accept or reject God's love for them. Remember, we are his representative.

So, what do you do when your beautiful, round-cheeked cherub turns into a self-willed, tantrum-rolling Tasmanian devil? Or when your innocent, sweet fifth-grader morphs into a rebellious preteen? This will be the true test of the genuineness of our (God's) love for them. Does your love for your children reveal conditional or unconditional love? What messages do your daily reactions to their disobedience convey? You can look to God to show you how to respond and how to speak in a way that consistently will plant seeds of his secure, unconditional love in their hearts. The forthcoming chapters on communication and discipline will discuss how we can speak in a way that conveys unconditional love. Your children need to know you love them beyond any conceivable agony they may put you through. This supernatural love will draw them to God's bosom.

The Way You Love

We communicate love to one another in different ways. The problem is that we do not realize we do! My tendency is to evaluate a person's love toward me by the way I show love to him or her. I am a communicator, so I like to talk at a deep relational level most of the time. To me, that says love; it says relationship. Not all my children enjoy talking at this level, so when one of them would say only the essentials of the needed information, I interpreted this as his/her not wanting to talk to me at all; that she didn't want to spend time with me or that he didn't really love me that much. This was one of my big parenting mistakes, because I would make it known that I was hurt, upset, or disappointed that they didn't want to talk more. My reaction would result in their being hurt and feeling unloved. They would feel as if they were not living up to my standard of love; therefore, it brought insecurities for them and in our relationship.

The way you love is partially predisposed by how you were loved by your parents and family when you were a child. The way you love is, to some degree, subject to your personality type too. You, as the parent, create the training ground for your child to learn what love looks like, just as your parents created that training ground for you.

How you were parented leaves a lasting impression and impacts how you relate to others in a relationship. I was raised by parents who had marital problems and a host of personal issues. They really did not know how to love in a way that would promote healthy relationships; therefore, I grew up not understanding what a healthy love relationship looked like. I learned how to love and be loved when I became a Christian and allowed God to love me and teach me how to love.

You might come from a home where your parents didn't bring up subjects that were uncomfortable or controversial. Maybe they were leery of being too authoritative or critical, and they failed to bring healthy confrontation to any problem areas of your life. To this day, you might be apprehensive about communicating negative feedback to someone close to you, because when you were growing up, you did not witness how to share negative things with love, grace, and understanding. Or maybe you grew up with parents who were harsh and critical, and that is the way you choose to communicate too. Regardless, we have the ability to change and grow.

God's love for us has nothing to do with how wonderful and loving we are at times, nor does he love us only because we are pleasurable to be with. God's love for us really lies with him. He is able to love us unconditionally because his fountain of love never dries up. Just ponder this for a moment: God contains all the love there is in this universe. He is the wellspring of love. When you think of God, you should think of love. It is as if the universe is pulsating waves of his love toward us as he cares for his creation. Because he is the wellspring of love, we can draw from him all the love we need to pour on our children, even if we were not raised or taught this type of love.

Filled with Love

Love is the most important aspect of God; it is the most important thing for us. Love is what makes everything work. I truly believe that the more you love God, the more you can love others. Loving God fills your heart with love. It is so much easier to love others when your heart is full of God's love. But to love God and to allow his love to penetrate you, you need to focus and meditate on his love for you. You need to read his words that talk about his love. You need to believe he loves you. For a sponge to absorb water, you need to place the sponge in the water and allow it to soak up the water. The same principle applies to absorbing God's love. You need to put yourself in the place where you can absorb his love—in prayer and his Word. You cannot be distracted and busy all the time and expect to always feel his love. You will build that love relationship with him by slowing down, spending time with him in prayer, and listening to him as you read the Bible.

This type of love is supernatural; it is spiritual. You get it from God, not from emotionally driven strategies or man-made vessels or even from other Christians. Their love is still tainted and diluted, because sin pollutes their love. When I want to give love to my children, I do not want it to be hand-me-down love. I need to get the love from God, who can give me love that is "100 proof," because by the time his love passes through me to my child, it will be polluted by my own sin. If I fill my heart with people's love, then I give my child hand-me-down love. Human love is not going to withstand all the relational hiccups to which unconditional love can hold up.

Love Generates Forgiveness

"Two men owed money to a certain moneylender. One owed him five hundred denarii and the other fifty. Neither of them had the money to pay him back, so he canceled the debts of both. Now which of them will love him more?" Simon replied, "I suppose the one who had the bigger debt canceled." "You have judged correctly," Jesus said. Then he turned toward the woman and said to Simon, "Do you see this woman? I came into your house. You did not give me any water for my feet, but she wet my feet with her tears and wiped them with her hair. You did not give me a kiss, but this woman, from the

time I entered, has not stopped kissing my feet. You did not put oil on my head, but she has poured perfume on my feet. Therefore, I tell you, her many sins have been forgiven ... for she loved much. But he who has been forgiven little loves little." Then Jesus said to her, "Your sins are forgiven" (Luke 7:41–48, NIV).

If you want to teach your children to love, then teach them to forgive others readily and sacrificially. You can show them what forgiveness looks like when you practically and verbally communicate forgiveness to them as they disobey or treat you in an unloving way. We all raise our voice to our children at times, not because we plan it but because we blow it at times and sin. I have found a great blessing in saying, "I'm sorry. Will you forgive me?" The blessing is that my children are eager to respond, "Yes, I will." It always reconnects our hearts after a disagreement. It also has been an example to them of their need to ask for forgiveness. On the other end of the stick, there have been times when I haven't asked for forgiveness. This has been an example to them of what not to do.

I love the portion in the above passage that says *"her many sins have been forgiven ... for she loved much."* When you think about this, don't you come to the conclusion that the more we choose to love others, the more we are able to grant them forgiveness, and the more likely they are to forgive us? It looks like God has a love economy here. Jesus goes on to say more about how love brings forgiveness: *"But he who has been forgiven little loves little."* I think this is true. When you think about a relationship where there has been little or no forgiveness granted, it affects the way he or she doesn't show love. Take a person like Tom, who was raised by parents who did not take the time to nurture and mentor him. Tom was not given or shown forgiveness when he disobeyed or disappointed his parents. In fact, his parents didn't notice much about Tom, except when he did something that irritated or angered them. He did his best to seek his parents' approval, but he could never attain it. Tom grew up not knowing how to really love others sacrificially, without any strings attachèd and without walls and boundaries. If we want our children to love God and us sacrificially and readily, then we need to possess and share this type of love.

The Quality of Love

(Supplementary questions for personal or group discussion)

1. Describe a particular time you uniquely experienced God's love through a difficult time in your life.
2. In John 21:15–18, Jesus asks Peter if he loves him with an *agapao* love. *Agapao* is the type of love with which God loves us; it is a deep, strong, sacrificial love. Peter tells Jesus that he loves him with a *phileo* love. *Phileo* love is more of a strong friendship love.
   - Which love do you feel for God?
   - What can you do this week that will deepen your love relationship with God?
3. According to 1 John 4:18, what is the opponent of love?
   - How has this opponent interfered with your love relationship with others or your child?
4. In what way is God asking you to demonstrate his love to your child today?
5. What hurt or frustration is there right now with one of your children?
   - What does God want you to do with that hurt or frustration that will benefit your child in the long run? (Find a verse to go along with your answer, if possible.)
6. Why do you doubt God's love for you in times of sorrow or trouble?

4

The Quality of Grace

But He gives a greater grace. Therefore it says, "God is opposed to the proud, but gives grace to the humble."
James 4:6
(NAS)

Children are unpredictable. You never know what inconsistency they're going to catch you in next.
—Franklin P. Jones

What makes Christianity different from all other religions is grace: the grace that God provided in giving us a Savior to take away the penalty of our sins, regardless of how horrible they are and how unworthy we are. It was a gift not earned on our own merit but freely given with a motive of loving kindness and favor.

In the realm of parenting, grace is the outcome of the favor and loving kindness you have toward each of your children. Grace comes in different levels and amounts, depending on the child and the situation. For example, you can apply more grace to a child who doesn't have the mental or physical ability to understand or perform something you are teaching him or training him. Or you can give less grace to a child who continually rebels and disobeys you, no matter how many consequences you dish out. Showing grace to your child can vary through the years; it can vary through difficult events in life; it can vary through the stages of maturity. The point is, we are to show them grace in varying degrees, according to what they need at any given time.

I have noticed that the amount of grace I gave my child sometimes depended on my disposition, such as how much I tried to control things or people in my life. For example, as a child, one of my sons was a very creative individual. If you have a child who is creative, you know that creativity usually encompasses all aspects of life—art, music, clothing. There were times when my son wore more jewelry than I would dream of wearing myself, when he had more hair than I had, and when he spent time crafting more than I had the time to do. He never wore makeup—the thought never entered his mind—but he did, on one occasion, color his nails black with a Sharpie.

I miss seeing his creativity—those days are long gone. Now he is busy focusing his time on his career and his marriage. At that time, I had a choice in my parenting to allow or disallow things that I didn't like—not things that were based on biblical principles but just based on my likes and dislikes. Even though I did make some decisions based on my preferences, most of the time I allowed my children to express themselves in the ways their personalities dictated. This came about from my favor and loving kindness toward them, which is in opposition to the desire to control the environment around me, which makes me feel comfortable and secure.

Favoring Your Child

Grace is an undeserved acceptance and love; it is favor. The Greek word for grace is *charis*, which is related to the word for joy or pleasure. *Charis* originally referred to something delightful or attractive in a person; something that brought pleasure to others. It refers to one's giving goodwill, loving kindness, and favor to another. Nothing speaks to our children more than their seeing that we find them delightful, appealing, and a pleasure to be with and that we desire to favor them with goodwill and loving kindness.

We have brought a few children into our home who needed to experience a normal family life. It has been a God-given privilege and assignment, as well as challenging and complicated at times. The first child we brought into our home was from Russia. Tanya (I am using a pseudonym to protect her privacy) was a young teenager when we first met her. By God's providence, she ended up on our front porch one day, lost. She had gotten off the bus and could not orient herself to the neighborhood to find her host family's house. She rang our doorbell, I opened the door, and she began explaining her dilemma in her thick Russian accent. I figured out which neighbor she was staying with and directed her to the house at the end of the street. Later that evening, our neighbor called and thanked us for helping Tanya. In the course of the conversation, my neighbor mentioned that they needed to find another host family for her because they were concerned she might have some negative influence on their own children—Tanya had broken a couple of trust issues with them. My heart began to feel a unique love and favor toward this girl. In fact, during that week, love for Tanya grew to such an extent that I knew I needed to share what was going on in my heart with my husband.

My husband and I began to pray about taking this teenage girl into our home to nurture and care for her. By the end of the week, my husband called my neighbor and offered to take Tanya into our home. She became a part of our family for about two years and then moved back to Russia to live with her mom.

Our time spent with her was mixed with joy and sorrow. There were huge adjustments and sacrifices in taking Tanya into our home—our family structure changed immediately because of the age, personality, and demeanor of that extra child. We had to spend an incredible amount of time building a relationship with her and help her work through the issues that brought her to need a home. Our own children had to sacrifice time with us, so we could spend more time with Tanya. In turn, we gave up time with our own children, so we could focus on making Tanya feel loved and part of the family. I still remember staying up until midnight at times, talking to her about her family relationships, her dreams, and how she missed home. Because she was the oldest child in our family, it changed the things we did as a family. Tanya was a teenager; our children were in grade school. So we had to adjust our standard family activities to be a bit more exciting for a teenager. It was a time when the whole family invested their lives in one person.

When we adopted Tanya into our hearts as a member of our family, it came with the same emotional labor as having our own child. The result of our time spent with Tanya was her having a deeper and cherished relationship with her mom when she returned to Russia and her having a new relationship with the Lord. God's grace seemed to bloom and explode in our hearts toward Tanya. We loved her with a special, unique love. I can only say that when God calls you to a specific purpose, he will shower you with everything you need to accomplish it.

God's thoughts toward us are not negative but full of joy. He accepts and loves us through his unmerited favor and grace toward us. The goodness of God causes him to find pleasure in giving his children undeserved gifts. God shows his goodness and favor toward us when we do not deserve it. In fact, grace shines forth brightly once we recognize the severity with which God could actually deal with us because of how sinful we truly are.

I want my children to see God's grace stamped in bold print all over me. I am a recipient of his saving grace. I have not arrived at being a Christian; what has arrived is Jesus in my heart. I am in awe of God's grace toward me when I recognize my need for his daily grace, because I continue to fall short of his standard of holiness. The more I recognize and experience God's grace in my life, the more I will recognize when my children need grace from me.

Share the Grace

When we ask God for forgiveness, we will experience his grace on a continual basis. I believe the result of recognizing and experiencing his grace daily will give us a thankful, humble attitude. This new attitude will produce an intense desire in us to share his grace with others and with our children. We will have a desire to see the impact that grace-sharing will have on others. If we can focus on increasing our grace-sharing with our family, then it will have a ripple effect, reaching out to our neighbors and others with whom we have contact. As they say, "Home is where the heart is," or should I say, "Home is where the heart is shown." Your family will be transformed by God's grace as you start pouring his grace upon their lives—as you begin to show them favor, to show them you love and accept them, despite their sinful behavior. Their thankful and humble attitudes will flourish and eventually, they will become grace-sharers themselves.

God is the owner of our lives. He gives with generosity to his children. God doesn't dish out blessings based on merit. He does not give us salvation based on merit. He gives blessings to us based on his grace toward us. He is generous. He blesses us far beyond what we deserve and what we think we have earned by Christian work or behavior. I have heard the old saying, "You can't outgive the giver." Matthew 20 tells us about a man who owned a growing, successful vineyard. It was time to pick his fruit for the season, so he went down to the marketplace, where he knew he would find men waiting for business owners to hire them for the day. He hired several men early that morning, with the agreement of paying them a denarius for a full day of work.

Throughout the day, the vineyard owner made several trips back to the marketplace and found more men who needed the work, and each time he hired them with the agreement of paying a denarius for the day's work. The last group of men he hired that day ended up only spending an hour of work time. This vineyard owner had such incredible care and compassion for these men, who needed the work to support their families, that he agreed to pay them for a full day's work. He really did not need the extra help but was concerned about their needs.

Your children need to witness the grace that God has given you. They need to see that no matter what they have done or not done, no matter how much they obey or disobey, it does not rob them of the generosity you have to bless them beyond what they deserve. I know what you are thinking: "Now, wait a minute … how do I give grace generously when I need to put my foot down on disobedience or attitude issues?" I say to that, emphatically, that grace does not nullify discipline. Giving grace does not mean you tolerate outright disobedience. Just as grace does not nullify the truth of God's standards of holiness, grace softens the punishment instead of giving the offender what he deserves.

When our son wanted to get a job after school, we bought a car for him to use. After a while of his having a car and a job, he began to abuse the privilege of independence in a way we highly disapproved of. We confronted him on the decisions he was making when he was using his car in his free time, and we warned him to stop it. He continued to use his freedom in the same way, so we decided to take away some of his free hours, insisting he spend that time at home instead. We had every right to take away the vehicle that gave him that freedom, but we felt that was too harsh, because he would have lost his job. We felt the anger he would have developed toward us would have had a ripple effect. Instead, we wanted to discipline him in a way that would break his heart, not break him. He knew there was a huge possibility that we could take his car away, but instead, he witnessed the grace we granted to him.

If I am aware of the grace I receive from God on a daily basis, I become humble before him. I know what I really deserve, but I ask for what I don't deserve.

Grace in Action

You give grace by showing Jesus to your children—by showing his character and values to them and letting them know that the truth of God's standard is here to protect and perfect all of us. Giving grace does not mean you give your children a "hall pass" for disobedience; it means having the attitude of Christ as you show them the standard and condition of obedience and disobedience. I think that is why it is imperative that you know the character of God as much as possible this side of heaven. How will you have his attitude and know his standards of holiness if you do not spend enough time getting to know him? If you don't spend time building a close relationship with him, then you will be apt to spout off the dos and don'ts of Christianity to your children, which definitely will not compel them to follow you—or him—with their hearts.

Grace does not lower the standards of holiness. It does not show grace to tolerate a sinful behavior or attitude in your child, to a degree that you do next to nothing about their sin—that compromises God's standards of holiness. Children need to understand what grace is by learning what sin is and what the penalty, or wages, of sin are in God's book (Romans 3:10, 23; Romans 6:23). At the same time, give your child the same grace you give yourself when you sin and need to go to the throne of grace for forgiveness.

Grace is not nit-picking every attitude or action they display. Do not confuse sinful behavior with the quirkiness of your child's personality. Understanding how your child communicates, verbally and nonverbally, will help you identify if the attitude or behavior is sinful or just a mark of his personality. We need to give our children some freedom to express themselves in the way their personality dictates. Some personalities are winsome; some are more serious and intense. Allow them to express themselves within their natural bents (without being disrespectful or disobedient). We don't want to make them conform to an image that we create. Sin is sin—it is spelled out in the Bible. It is not fair, loving, or gracious to make up our own rules of attitudes and behaviors, and call it sin.

Pick and choose how big you are going to make the mountains of disagreements. Molehill-sized disagreements are much easier to work with in children's hearts. If their actions indicate a character issue, then help them see it, or at least find out if it is really a character issue or simply an innocent desire that has absolutely nothing to do with pride, lust, vanity, or other sin that could lurk behind the word or action.

Grace is not adding your rules to God's rules. I would tell my kids this decision or desire was based on a God rule or a house rule. A house rule was my personal preference for the way things were done or said in our home. For example, I would not allow the children to say "shut up." I disliked that phrase because I heard it many times in my home when I was a child. Maybe one of your house rules would be no TV past a certain time, no dating, no tattoos, or no junk food. But when making house rules, take into consideration how much you will exasperate your children with numerous and strict house rules. Don't bring God into the picture; if it is not spelled out in scripture, don't claim it is God's rule.

Grace does not nullify discipline and training. Hebrews 12:7, 9, and 11 talk about God training by discipline and that it will produce peace in our hearts and lives, because it looks and lives in righteousness. Our children have a bent to sin, just as we do, but it is up to us to give them a reason and purpose *not* to be overcome or taken captive by their sin. If we can model a life of peace and grace, mixed with purpose and righteousness, then we have something to offer them that will help direct them to God, who will protect them from themselves.

There are times when they will question your faith and question their own faith. At these times, give them grace as they share their struggles, disappointments, confusion, and disagreements. If you limit their opportunities to talk with you about the struggles concerning their faith, it will eventually silence them from sharing openly and honestly. If they say they do not know if they believe in what you believe, allow them to share their thoughts. Then tell them you understand how hard it is to walk a life of faith. Pray for them and continue to show undeserved love and grace to them. Don't give them the impression that they don't belong or that something is desperately wrong with them. Instead, coach and coax them back into or toward their faith.

I question the extent to which some parents exercise "tough love." They use it in an extreme measure when they dish out unemotional, ungracious words and actions toward their children, in order to get them to shape up. Tough love does not always look like grace; it can look like conditional love. Applying discipline because of outright disobedience is not tough love; it is training them to obey.

But even discipline has its limit before it turns into conditional tough love. Love is very sacrificial. It is giving up your personal desires, personal timing, personal convictions (not God's commandments), and personal expectations for the sake of that person's spiritual growth. It is looking at God's grace, which you have received and are still receiving, and being willing to dish out the same portion of grace to your child. Grace is being patient and long-suffering when you think you don't deserve the pain of the situation or struggle it has become.

Grace is not expecting your children to be perfect or anywhere near perfect. They are going to sin many, many times. They will not like what you say or demand from them. If you expect sin, disobedience, and foolish behavior from your children, then you will not be disappointed or distraught every time things don't go right. Their relationship with you will hinge on how you react to their independent and rebellious behavior. If they see you standing by them, loving them, while not supporting their behavior, they will be more likely to grab your hand when they have had enough of themselves and the consequences of their decisions.

Jesus said in Matthew 11:28–30: "*Come to Me, all who are weary and heavy laden ... take My yoke upon you and learn from Me ... For My yoke is easy and My burden is light*" (NAS). God's standard of holiness should not be made a burden or a weight of discouragement to our children; rather, it should be a compass for them to follow God's path of righteousness and see that is the only path that ultimately will be fulfilling and productive. As they walk this path and stumble and trip at times, they need to be reassured that they are loved and accepted by you and him, continually.

As we were dealing with our son's disobedience, we made it clear that we did not accept his behavior, but we did love and accept him and that he was still adored and cherished by us and God.

The Quality of Grace
(Supplementary questions for personal or group discussion)

1. What house rules have you instituted that are based solely on your preferences and not on any moral or lawful principle?
    - Do you notice any unreasonable frustration, anger, or disrespect from your child regarding any of the house rules you listed?
    - Are there any house rules that could be negotiated?
2. How can you tell if your child recognizes that you find her delightful and a pleasure to be with?
3. Think of an area of disobedience or sin that your child is in right now. How can you communicate both your disapproval and grace to him/her at the same time?
    - What would you say and/or do?
4. Do you believe you have given enough grace to your child? If not, what can you do to change that this week?
5. How can you teach your child to respect your preferences and respect God's commands and principles?
6. How has God's grace changed the way you love others?

5
The Quality of Patience

And the Lord's bond-servant must not be quarrelsome, but be kind to
all, able to teach, patient when wronged, with gentleness correcting
those who are in opposition, if perhaps God may grant them
repentance leading to the knowledge of the truth, and they may come
to their senses and escape from the snare of the devil, having been
held captive by him to do his will.
2 Timothy 2:24–26
(NAS)

Raising kids is part joy and part guerilla warfare.

—Ed Asner

By nature, I am not a patient person. So it would stand to reason that God would use the personality of my second child to teach me how to become patient. My middle child was a very quiet child, but on the inside, his mind was busy making all kinds of suggestions as to what he could do to create the most chaos. His intentions were never to stress me out but only to appease his curiosity and engineering abilities. I did my best to keep from his reach certain tools, hardware, utensils, or anything else he could imagine using to undo or adjust pieces of furniture or other things. But as you would guess, with pure, raw determination, he got a hold of whatever he needed to do his handiwork.

I will never forget the day I was closing the bathroom door and noticed it didn't feel right. Upon closer inspection, I saw the door brackets were undone and the screws were on the floor. Seriously, I have no idea where he found the screwdriver he needed to do the job—he was only about three or four years old. I watched him like a hawk, but apparently I underestimated him and took my eyes and attention off him too long at times.

Aside from the time he took out all the screws in his brother's crib (thankfully, his brother was not in it at the time), the most embarrassing and horrifying time was when I had a friend over, who had two sweet little girls. She and I were upstairs visiting, when we heard pounding downstairs in the playroom. As I walked down the stairs, I thought to myself, *It is probably nothing more than my son hammering with his little red plastic hammer on the wall.* Obviously, I wasn't thinking clearly. When I finally caught view of my precious one, his little red plastic hammer was not in his hand. Instead, he held a full-size metal hammer—my friend's two sweet little girls stood next to him in total awe of his great ability. I can only imagine he felt quite grown up in front of two admirers. Obviously, I quickly grabbed the hammer from his hand. Just about that time, my friend arrived on the scene. I was frustrated with my son because he yet again had gone beyond the boundaries of what to play with, and I was embarrassed because of my lack of parenting skills (to keep my child obedient and out of trouble). I responded with exasperation and even started to cry.

Now that I look back, I think it is rather funny and typical. I had an intelligent, engineering son, who thought he needed the big-boy tools to do the job right. It was really I who needed the parenting. I needed to accept the uniqueness of my son and apply patience in training and pruning his exuberance and lack of discernment. But what was going on inside of me was an intolerance and shame of his behavior, which materialized in impatience. My visible impatience made my son feel ashamed, made me look like a bad parent, and made my friend uncomfortable. I could have simply told my son to never use big-people tools again. I could have told him he would be disciplined after our guests left for getting into Daddy's tools again. And I could have apologized to my friend for my son's behavior and shared that I was still in the training process of reigning in his big-boy mentality. But I didn't.

Now, however, I am more mature and understanding of children, which earns my title of Grandma.

Patience Has Its Purpose

It seems one of the ways we can lose some ground in parenting is when we lose our patience with our children. Even though we may do many things right in our daily parenting, it just takes that one time when we lose it with our kids. Even if we try to hide our impatience, they see it. Believe me—they see it. I think that is why toddlers are so good at getting their way at times; they can detect our weaknesses. They see when we are wearing down. When we lose our temper, we also lose some of the respect and authority in our child's eyes. Put a patient, persistent, consistent parent in front of them, and you will see them eventually realize that the jig is up. God is that type of parent—patient, persistent, and unchanging. Eventually, we are the ones who do the changing.

When you think about God's patience with his nation, Israel, and his patience with mankind, you may realize that God had a just reason to punish his children when they showed little respect for his authority, when they rebelled outright against his rule, and when they disobeyed direct commands. However, God usually gave them his gift of patience—at least initially—so that through his patience, they would be led to repentance.

This is God's goal in showing us patience. *"God's patience is slow to anger in regards to our disobedience, our sin"* (Psalm 86:15). Through his kindness and forbearance, we are led to repentance (Romans 2:4). When Israel disappointed or irritated him, he continued to apply patience, discipline, and guidance, without indicating that he would ever disown or not love them. He always showed them there was a better way to take in life. Just think about God's goal in his patience toward us—our repentance. I would say this is quite a compelling reason for us to use the same approach with our children, hoping to reach the same result.

Patience Portrayed

Being patient is definitely not a passive undertaking. According to one definition from the *New Bible Dictionary*, it is "restraint in face of opposition or oppression." As I read the definitions of patience from various resources, I found that it carries the idea of enduring the sufferings of life, such as some of the wrongs done to us or the painful actions of others. It is the endurance, the waiting for things to improve or be restored; it is being steadfast in the midst of a trial, maintaining our faithfulness to God and others.

We are to imitate God's patience with others. As we receive, we are to give. We are to be slow to anger when wronged and to have endurance in adversity. We are to be steadfast as we wait on God to fulfill his purpose in the situation. We show our love to others through the action of patience.

In patience, we can bear, hope, and endure all things. First Corinthians 13:4, 7 describe for us how we show love through our patience: "*Love is patient, love is kind ... love bears all things, believes all things, hopes all things, endures all things.*" To bear something, to hope in something, and to endure something requires patience, and patience relies on love to produce it. Without love being the heartbeat, how will we produce genuine patience with others? Yes, we can manufacture patience and other character qualities, but how long we maintain it is the proof of the real deal. Exodus 34:6 describe God as the "*Lord, the Lord God, compassionate and gracious, slow to anger, and abounding in loving-kindness and truth.*" God is able to be patient with us because love abounds in him toward us.

I found the definition of forbearance in *Webster's Dictionary* to be very practical for applying patience to parenting. Forbearance (a synonym of patience) is defined as "a refraining from the enforcement of something (as a debt, right, or obligation) that is due. It is the act of forbearing: patience."[2] When we forbear a situation with our child, we essentially withhold the punishment that she may deserve. It is refraining from retaliating or punishing, which then produces the action of patience. Let me break it down in practical terms. *Webster's* defines patient as

- bearing pains or trials calmly or without complaining;
- manifesting forbearance under provocation or strain;
- not hasty or impetuous;
- steadfast despite opposition, difficulty, or adversity; and
- able or willing to bear.[3]

Let's take those five definitions and break them down even further. Look again at the first definition of patient. Calm means free from agitation, excitement, or disturbance. Our own emotions will always feed into another person's emotion. Any emotion you choose to show, such as agitation, will direct your child's response to you. It will either compound the issue or minimize the situation. The last thing I want is to cause my child to become more emotional than she already is, so I need to take the precautions to not be overly emotional myself.

The word complaining means to express grief, pain, or discontent; it is to make a formal accusation or charge. Usually, when we get agitated, it is seen in our expression but also by our words. Showing patience to our children means we do not verbalize how much they irritate us or cause us grief. Sharing with them some of the worry their behavior or attitude has caused us can be good and profitable, if done at the right time and in a loving way. But be careful not to put the entire blame on them. We are responsible for our own thoughts and actions toward them and the situation at hand.

Patient means "refraining in light of being provoked." That means when your child is pushing your buttons or trying your patience, you are to respond with the attitude of calmness and not be hasty.

Take your time in deciding what you are going to do in response to his/her disobedience, remarks, or attitude. Obviously, there will be times when you'll need to respond quickly, when you probably have decided beforehand what your response is going to be each time your child disobeys or gives you an attitude. The point is, are those times of response getting the best of you or getting the best out of the situation?

It comes down to being "steadfast despite all the opposition, difficulty, or adversity." Keeping steady and predictable in how you relate to your children eventually will give them the assurance that you really mean what you say and will follow through with any conditional promises. *"With all humility and gentleness, with patience, showing forbearance to one another in love"* (Ephesians 4:2). Being patient with "one another" applies to your children, too. We tend to not think of our children as people when they are young, but they are. They also start out as nonbelievers. What better reason to show them the grace of patience in order to lead them to repentance (Romans 2:4).

Proverbs gives us a couple of principles that should make us mindful in applying patience to our parenting. Proverbs 14:29 says, *"Whoever is slow to anger has great understanding, but he who has a hasty temper exalts folly."* Proverbs 15:18 says, *"A hot-tempered person stirs up strife, but he who is slow to anger quiets contention."* These are two great verses to put to memory if you struggle with words flying off your lips with great velocity and ferocity! Remember your destination, your plan, and your purpose in parenting: evangelism and discipleship. Through showing our children the patience of God, we will direct them to their need of repentance.

The Quality of Patience
(Supplementary questions for personal or group discussion)

1. What situation with your child brings out the most impatience in you?
    *   Why do you think it exhausts your patience?
2. What are some reasons that God calls us to be patient servants, according to 2 Timothy 2:24–26?
3. From the five definitions for patient listed in this chapter, which area of growth is needed in your parenting right now?
4. Can you explain one area where God has shown his repeated patience to you?
    *   How has God's patience with this issue made you feel about yourself, and how does it make you feel about him?
5. Would your family call you a patient person? Why or why not?

Part Three
How We Understand Each Other:

The Way We Communicate Love, Grace, and Patience
Our Expression of Affection
Our Distinguishing Personality

6

The Way We Communicate Love, Grace, and Patience

The unfolding of your words gives light; It gives understanding to the
simple.
Psalm 119:130
(NAS)

Always end the name of your child with a vowel, so that when you yell,
the name will carry.

—*Bill Cosby*

This message was seen on a church sign: "We care about you, Sundays 10 a.m. only."⁴ Although this church expressed that it cares about people, the words and the way they are conveyed produced something else. Communicating something clearly can be difficult sometimes. Communicating is sharing your feelings, thoughts, intentions, philosophy, opinions, and/or innermost desires. You are sending a message through what you say, how you say it, and why you say it.

As you communicate to your child, you are teaching him to communicate back to you and how to communicate to people in his life—friends, family, teachers, neighbors, future coworkers, and future mate. When you communicate to your child, you express who you are, what you want, what you like and dislike, and what your beliefs and values are.

The more you talk with your child at this interactive level, the better he will know you, and in turn, it will cause him to reveal more things about himself. It is an opportunity for him to express his thoughts and desires to you. Parents need to coax thoughts out of their children—usually, children don't openly express their innermost thoughts and feelings. You want to understand and know your children's hearts. Helping them express their thoughts helps them understand what is in their own hearts and what they really desire and want. It can help them see they need to allow Christ to rule their hearts, too.

You can begin having these heart-to-heart conversations with your children at an early age. Ask them what they like and dislike and why they like or dislike it. Use their wants and desires to help them see what is in their hearts. This also will help them understand what is behind another person's wants and desires.

Let me give you an example: Say your child witnesses another child at school bullying someone, or maybe it is your child who is doing the bullying. You can help your child understand (but not accept) the possible reasons why this child is bullying other children. Ask your child, "Why do you think he is acting that way? What is he trying to show people? What could be some reasons?" At this point in your conversation, you could suggest reasons why people bully. For example, perhaps they don't have any freedom at home so they want to control someone else, or they live in a home that is unhappy or angry all the time. Or maybe they believe no one likes them, so they become angry about it. What would help them not to bully and yet get that desire met?

You might need to change the words, but the point is to ask questions that will reveal the possible motive and desire a person has behind his or her actions or words. Your goal is not to teach your child to judge others unfairly but to learn to understand the possible reasons for people's behaviors or attitudes.

Words of Life or Death

Communication is not just what you say but how you say it and why you say it. God calls us his ambassadors; we represent him as we communicate and relate to others. He has a job for us to fulfill in our relationships with one another, so we better learn how to communicate his way. This means setting aside our own motives and desires before we choose the words we utter. Our words should carry out God's goal in the relationship.

Words influence others, whether the influence is good or bad. What we say influences another to think or act in a certain way. The desires and motives in our heart direct our tongue to speak them into being. We want to realign those desires and motives into Christ's desires and motives for ourselves and for the other person to whom we are speaking. If we do not realign our desires into a godly desire, we will speak words that might be self-centered and unloving. Self-centered talk is part of that "unwholesome talk" that is mentioned in Ephesians 4:29. It is poor quality and unfit for use. It is speech that reflects our selfishness, arrogance, and idols.

According to God, as stated in Ephesians 4:29, we are to speak in a way that will "benefit those who listen." This is an undertaking of the Holy Spirit in each of our lives. It cannot be done in the flesh on a continual basis. Oh, sure, we can control our tongue for a given period of time, but sooner or later, the wellspring of our heart (motives and desires) is going to burst forth and come out of our mouth. A daily submission to the Holy Spirit can enable us to sift out the anger, frustration, sadness, fear, envy, greed, resentment, anxiety, and expectations from the wellspring of our heart.

How do we speak in a way that "benefits" the other person? We have the opportunity to "add to" something in the other person's life when we talk to him/her. We can add good things or evil things to that person's life. We can speak words of life or speak words of death.

Let's take nagging as an example. Would you say that if your spouse or relative nags you to change or to do something, it makes you feel like jumping up and doing it? Probably not. It makes me feel like giving up or retreating. So in a sense, it produces death in me; it discourages me, or it can make me feel worthless.

Proverbs 18:21 says, *"Death and life are in the power of the tongue"* (NAS). These words of life are associated with God; words of death are just the opposite. In fact, we can say words of death are Satan's language. Any thoughts that have turned into words that will produce destruction, deception, lies, ill intentions, turmoil, hurt, pain, or anguish are words of death. Any thoughts that have turned into words that will produce or promote hope, peace, love, joy, restoration, redemption, compassion, healing, and spiritual growth are words of life. These words of life are spoken in truth, without being deceptive or manipulative in any way.

Speaking words of life means speaking God's truth to a person; it also means speaking in a way that reveals your care and concern for that person. Speak words that are patient, kind, humble, gracious, peaceful, and forgiving—words that will protect and are trustworthy, hopeful, and steadfast (1 Corinthians 13:4–7).

Speaking words of truth is essential in a relationship, but it is all in how and why we choose to say them. What is my intention? What do I hope to accomplish when I speak the truth to this person? Will it produce good or evil? Is my desire selfish, or am I looking out for the person's best interest? Am I speaking out of my own expectations and demands or from God's desires for this person? God's desire is always to reveal himself to us and to sanctify us (mature us, to become more like Christ) to be ambassadors for him.

Talk the Walk

The best way to teach your child to communicate biblically and correctly is for you to learn to communicate better. You need to show them how to speak in a way that will promote healthy relationships. You can practice the principles of speaking words of life, instead of speaking words of death to your child. You can become more purposeful in your conversations by asking your child questions about how and why he feels and thinks about something. You also can put to memory these six words to help you communicate biblically. Communicate the following to your children:

- love (for each other)
- respect (for them and you)
- authority (learning to come under authority)
- compassion (understanding of their feelings and yours)
- dialogue (a two-way relationship, not dictatorship)
- resolution (how to solve disagreements and sinful actions)

Let's look at the use of some of these principles in a typical situation with a younger child. You can adjust the words to an older child or teenager. The point is to clearly communicate.

You ask your child to pick up the toys because playtime is over. She becomes angry (passively or aggressively). You say, "I understand you are angry because you have to pick up your toys. You will be able to continue playing with your toys after naptime." (This gives her your understanding and compassion and shows your authority.) She is hesitant in picking up the toys. You say, "I would like you to pick up your toys. Will you pick up your toys for Mommy?" (This gives her a choice to respond.) "Thank you for obeying Mommy." (This shows gratitude and respect.) You can add. "That shows me you love me."

What if she says no to the choice you gave her? Then you need to show your authority by issuing a command with calmness and peace. (If your child is younger than two, make sure it is outright and intentional disobedience and not her just thinking out loud or mimicking.)

You say, "I asked you to pick up your toys. Pick up your toys now, please." (Kneel down and look into her eyes. She will get the picture.) You can give her a choice to obey or be disciplined. If she says no again, discipline her by taking away a toy for a while, send her to her room, spank, give her a chore, or send her to the time-out chair.

After discipline, say, "Next time I ask you to pick up your toys, will you obey Mommy?" (Say it with love and tenderness, yet firmness.)

In this scenario, you are communicating your desire for the child to obey. As the parent, you are communicating your expectations. You are communicating it with love, with authority, with compassion, with respect, and with the expectation to resolve the conflict.

A little side note: as you train your child to obey, as shown in the above scenario, you may want to initially give her a few opportunities to choose to obey. But eventually, you will want to train her to obey upon the first request.

The parent in this scenario is teaching her child to respond properly, with respect and self-control. We want to take time to teach our children to love and respect others and to learn how to minimize and resolve conflicts in their relationships. I believe this helps them build emotional stability. It helps them learn to adjust and maintain their emotions as they dialogue with you and others. They will learn to understand people better, understand the twists and turns of relationships, and understand there is a purpose in relationships.

The way we express our thoughts, desires, and beliefs to our children will impact how they view God and Christians. I want my children to experience communication from me that is filled with "life words." I want them to desire God's truth above all other things. Although I will mess up by speaking "words of death" at times, my desire is to always point my children to Christ as I share those thoughts, desires, and beliefs. I need to remember to measure my words (before I speak them) with my desire to point my children to Christ.

The Way We Communicate
Love, Grace, and Patience
(Supplementary questions for personal or group discussion)

1. How would you describe the way you usually communicate? (Use verbs and adverbs.)
2. What questions could you ask your child that would give you a picture of how he views his life today/this week?
3. What does ungodly speech look like, according to Ephesians 4:29–32?
   - Look up each descriptive word in *Webster's Dictionary* and define it.
   - What is the opposite of each descriptive word you used to describe ungodly speech?
4. What are three things God calls us to be in Ephesians 4:32?
   - Using *Webster's Dictionary*, define each word.
5. Why do you think verse 32 is the solution to verse 31?

7
Our Expression of Affection

Be devoted to one another in brotherly love; give preference to one another in honor; not lagging behind in diligence, fervent in spirit, serving the Lord ...
Romans 12:10–11
(NAS)

Children are like wet cement. Whatever falls on them makes an impression.

—*Dr. Haim Ginott*

Two of my sons are two years apart in age. They look alike, but they are so different in personality, style, and talents. For example, one likes to sleep with the blinds shut; the other, with the blinds open. One likes cheese; the other doesn't. One likes doing things with his hands; the other would rather be at a desk. One likes to dress conservatively; the other with splashes of personality. They also express their love in different ways. When I was raising them, it was difficult for me to grasp why they didn't express their affection toward me in the same way I expressed love to both of them, but one constantly gave me hugs and kisses, while the other chose to sit next to me and cuddle but gave very few kisses or hugs. The contrast in the way these two boys expressed love was so distinct, I thought I had done something wrong in the way I was loving them. As I mentioned in chapter three, one of the most useful things I learned in parenting my children is the way they showed love to me. Later on, I came across a book by Dr. Gary Chapman, *The Love Languages*,[5] which describes in detail what I noticed with my own children. I love his book and the way Dr. Chapman fully explains all variations of our love languages.

Basically, learning your child's love language is all about how he/she receives and expresses love. Study how your child shows his love toward you, and it probably will reveal how he would like you to love him back. Understanding how each of my children showed love helped me from getting hurt when they didn't show love the way I thought they should have. Even today, now that my children are grown, I refer back to the way they choose to show love, so that I don't misread it and get my feelings hurt or think they don't love me as much as they used to.

Dr. Gary Chapman suggests there are five love languages:

- words of affirmation
- quality time
- gifts
- acts of service
- physical touch

Tell Me How Great I Am

When my daughter became engaged, my husband I had her and her fiancé take a test to find out their individual love languages. It shocked me when I found out that my daughter's love language was "words of affirmation." Finding this out made me sad—I knew I hadn't focused on affirming the things she did when I was raising her. I tended to focus on helping her to become better at things, so I would instruct her more often than I would affirm what she had done. Back then, I now realize, what she needed was for me to say positive and complimentary things about her and her abilities. She needed more appreciation for her actions or simply for just how nice she looked that day. She was always telling her friends why she liked something about them and why she appreciated something they did.

The key point of this particular love language is to use many words to show your love. But there can be a downside to giving compliments or showing appreciation, and that is when you give someone too much positive talk. The person will begin to tune it out or not take it seriously. Also, if you give children a constant dose of praise, you can set them up for deflation later when someone criticizes them. I think if we are sincerely giving affirmation to our children in an appropriately balanced way, we will not be overly zealous and give too much positive talk. Be conscious of the manner in which you give your "words of affirmation," such as your tone of voice, your expression, and your body language. If I get in the habit of praising my child for something on a regular basis, my words and expression can become mechanical and empty. Words of affirmation convey encouragement for doing the right thing; they convey that you love and adore who your child is inside. Give meaning to your praise by making sure you praise her for the right reason, rather than just building her self-esteem with insincere compliments.

Hang Out with Me

My son has the love language of "quality time." He loves spending time with someone in a one-to-one setting, but it's not just spending time hanging out—he wants to spend quality time. Enjoying quality time means setting time aside for that person so you can spend time talking about things of importance. You like to share your feelings and the details that surround your life. Likewise, you like to listen to another person share her feelings and all the details of her life. Some people who have this love language enjoy inviting people to participate in an activity together, such as golf, tennis, shopping, road trips, or hitting garage sales. Regardless of the activity you may do together, you enjoy spending quality time and making memories together. If your child has this language of love, then spending time with her shows how important she is to you. Take the time to sit with her on the floor, playing or looking at something together. Spend some time with her doing favorite activities. If you have several children, try to set time aside with each one on a weekly basis. Do not drive yourself crazy by trying to do it on a daily basis. If you have three children, you could set aside Monday, Wednesday, and Friday for each individual child.

Give Me Something

"Receiving gifts" is another love language. It is easy to tell if a person uses this love language—he/she is always giving you something, whether homemade or store-bought. A person with this love language is thrilled when someone takes the time and effort to give him something as well. I love giving gifts; the problem is, my budget doesn't like it! When I am out shopping I always see something that I would like to buy for a particular person, because it shouts his/her personality to me, or it reminds me of that person. For me, giving gifts shows people I am thinking about them, I appreciate them, and I love them. It may not be an expensive gift, but I hope they recognize the thought behind the gift—that matters the most. The gift, however small or large, is a token of my love and appreciation for them. When I receive a gift from someone, it makes me feel like I am special to the person who gave it to me. It doesn't matter what the gift is; it is knowing this person has thought about me and wants to let me know she cares about me. If you have a child who seems to always give you something he made, or you see him sharing his things with other children, he might be using the love language of "receiving gifts."

Help Me

One of my sons has the love language of "acts of service." I can make him really happy by doing things for him—physical help, running errands, making a meal, shopping for him, and on occasion, cleaning things for him. Anything I can do for him with my hands, feet, or car shows him that I appreciate him.

If your child frequently asks you to help him with certain projects or asks you to do things for him, and in turn, he frequently asks if he can help you, then he might be exercising this love language.

Hold My Hand

Another of my sons has "physical touch" as a love language. As a child, he usually was holding my hand, hugging me, or giving me a kiss. This was unlike my other son, who didn't see the need to give his mother much physical affection to prove he loved her. Both sons, to this day, still show love to me in the same love language they used as children.

When physical touch is one of your love languages, you have a need to be touched in any form. It can be a hug, a tap on the shoulder, a kiss on the cheek, or a simple touch to the arm. You feel loved and accepted when people touch you. You tend to touch people when you talk with them. It is easy to tell when children have this love language—they cannot seem to get enough hugs and kisses from you. In fact, most of the time, they are the ones who initiate the hugs and kisses. They are more loving and affectionate to their siblings as well, which can be an irritant to the sibling who does not particularly enjoy that form of love language.

Love Factors

Other factors wire us to love others in our unique way; the way our parents raised us can be a huge factor. Think for a moment how your parents showed love to you. What love language would you assign to your mom? What about your dad? Do you think your parents loved you in the way you love to be loved? If your parents didn't quite meet the love quota of your particular love language, it probably affected the way you show love to others. The way our parents choose to communicate their love, their disapproval, anger, joy, and appreciation all has residual effects on us, like it or not. Our parents were not perfect and neither are we, as parents. We can learn from our parents' mistakes as well as from our own.

I know that my stubbornness hinders me from using the love language a person may prefer. It takes more work and sacrifice on my part to go the extra mile to love that person in his/her way. I can be intolerant of someone who claims I haven't shown her that I love her. What goes through my mind is something like this: "What do you mean I haven't shown you I love you? I did this! I did that!" I need to remind myself to step back and take a good long look at why that person feels that way. More often than not, it is my lack of understanding of how she *perceived* my love than my intentionally not loving her.

Another reason we may overlook someone's love language is if we are a bit too self-absorbed, self-centered, and self-focused. You see the "self" commonality? We can be so involved with ourselves and our life that we become insensitive to how another person may perceive our love. I know some Christians who walk around as if they're wearing a T-shirt with "Me" emblazoned on it—they talk only about themselves and do not take the time or energy to know others at a personal level. Sure, they say they care about and love others, but they demonstrate it poorly. Unfortunately, I can be just as guilty of being too self-absorbed at times.

Although we can learn to love our children in their unique love language, we also can be an example for them in how we love others. Teaching our children about these love languages will help them appreciate the different ways people show and receive love. It will encourage them to love beyond their natural tendency and to love sacrificially.

Our Expression of Affection
(Supplementary questions for personal or group discussion)

1. Make a list of each of your children's love languages.
2. What do you think is your dominant love language? What is your second love language?
3. What adjustments do you need to make in showing each child love in the way he/she receives and responds best?
4. What love language would you assign to your mom and dad when they were raising you and showing love to you as a child?
   - What effects do you think your parents had on your ability to show love to others (positive and negative)?
5. In what ways can you improve on loving others?
6. Make a list of ways love is shown from scripture passages that teach love. (Use a concordance or Bible dictionary to help you find passages on love.)

8
Our Distinguishing Personality

O Lord, you have searched me and known me! ... You search out my path and my lying down and are acquainted with all my ways. ... I praise you, for I am fearfully and wonderfully made.
Psalm 139:1, 3, 14
(ESV)

It's beauty that captures your attention; personality, which captures your heart.

—*Anonymous*

We all are born with a personality temperament that highly influences how we think and act. The four temperaments are *sanguine* (extroverted, fun-loving, persuasive, and optimistic), *choleric* (extroverted, strong-willed, independent, and opinionated), *phlegmatic* (introverted, calm, easygoing, and practical), and *melancholy* (introverted, dependable, analytical, and creative). I would have made fewer mistakes in parenting if I had understood my children's different styles of personalities. If I had been introduced to these four basic temperaments, I would have studied them and tried to match them to each of my children. I would have been able to understand my children better and, in turn, parent them from the viewpoint of how they saw and felt things in life. It was not until my children were in their late elementary school years that I learned about the different personality temperaments. But once I understood more about their temperaments, a huge door opened that enabled me to love better and parent better (not that I didn't continue to make big mistakes in parenting).

Understanding each of my children's temperaments—the ugly and beautiful side of their personalities—enabled me to see life through their way of thinking. I have been able to teach them about themselves and each other and how to deal with each of their strengths and weaknesses. I absolutely enjoyed and cherished getting to know them with more clarity as I filtered their behaviors through their unique personalities. This knowledge of their temperaments gave me even more reason to apply grace to their lives.

We may be dominant in one or two temperaments or sometimes three. Most of the time, a person has one dominant temperament along with a second temperament that complements the dominant. The third is often a weaker one that is seen periodically. Usually, there is no sign of a fourth temperament.

I would highly recommend investigating the four personality types. There are books and a lot of information on the Internet about them. *Spirit-Controlled Temperament* by Tim LaHaye, and *Personality Plus for Parents* by Florence Littauer are two excellent books.

Identifying your own temperament (online tests are available that determine temperament types) will help you become a better parent. You will be able to identify your strengths and weaknesses, which will give you an opportunity to grow in these areas. If your child is young, it will be difficult to determine positively his unique personality, but as he grows older, you likely will be able to pinpoint the temperaments. Let me share with you a quick snapshot of these four temperaments as I saw them in my own children as they were growing up.

The Personality That Loves Life

My daughter showed the traits of a sanguine and phlegmatic personality when I was raising her. Later on in life, I saw her melancholy side become stronger. As a sanguine child, however, she loved adventure and was very social. She often had dirt or food on her clothes from living life a bit too fast and carefree. She found enjoyment in nearly everything she did. She also often forgot about her responsibilities (including homework) and had a difficult time applying organization skills to her life.

The sanguine is super-sensitive to correction and criticism that is not given in a gracious and loving tone. This can be tough for a parent who has many responsibilities and tends to give out orders and corrections quickly, without carefully chosen words. Since a sanguine is forgetful and somewhat unorganized, this creates a challenge for a parent to graciously correct and remind a sanguine concerning her responsibilities. If you are aware of how your child filters words through her temperament when you speak in an ungracious and unloving manner, then you will likely adjust your tone and words.

The Personality That Loves Peace

I believe all of my children have phlegmatic as their secondary temperament. The phlegmatic is an easygoing personality; he is generally laid back and relaxed about life. A phlegmatic is seen as a peacemaker or sometimes a people pleaser. He is very loving and kind to people. A phlegmatic needs encouragement to move toward a goal and then to keep progressing toward the goal. He seems to be happy and content with where he is in life. Occasionally, however, he needs a boost from someone to get him motivated to do or change something. He tends to lean toward less work and effort. One of his greatest virtues is patience.

The Personality That Loves to Think

My son's dominant temperament is melancholy. I particularly enjoy this temperament, because it is one of my temperaments. My son is very analytical and methodical in his thinking—this was the case even as a very young child. I could always see him thinking, sitting silently with a serious face, as he looked at objects and people. He was not an overly "smiley" baby or child; he was more serious and purposeful in whatever he was doing. He also could figure out things faster than any of my other children. Melancholies see below the surface of things; they tend to feel deeper and see things with a deeper understanding. They also can help others identify and understand life and relationships better, because they can dive to the depths of another person's emotion or pain. They are highly sensitive people; therefore, they get their feelings hurt easily. After the choleric, a melancholy tends to be more critical and judgmental than the other temperaments. They can be overly emotional and pessimistic. On the brighter side, they can be very artistic and creative.

The Personality That Loves to Lead

The choleric temperament is defined mostly by leadership qualities—the choleric takes the lead in everything. He wants to get the job done quickly. It really doesn't matter if it is done perfectly; what matters is that there is something to conquer or fix. One of my sons has this temperament. He is great at finding a solution to any problem. If you don't agree with the solution, he will try to convince you it is the right solution. He does not like life to be boring, mundane, or predictable. He dreams big and is always finding ways to make life more fulfilling and exciting.

Cholerics tend to be insensitive to hurting people. They can unintentionally run over people with their words and actions, because they don't want to stop and think about the other person's feelings— they are too busy getting the job done or convincing others of their idea.

The Importance of Understanding Temperaments

There are strengths and weaknesses with each of these four temperaments. Learning more about these four temperaments will help you identify the areas in your child's temperament that need to be nurtured. Understanding your child's unique temperaments can help you evaluate when he is responding out of his temperament or something else. Watch how he responds to things, to people, and to problems. Is he responding out of his temperament, environment, fatigue, or stress? For example, if he is quiet and shy, doesn't like to rock the boat, and doesn't want any attention put on him, ask yourself why he is so compliant. Why is he so shy and timid? Is this part of his temperament? Or is he secure in who he is? Is he secure in your love? If these are weaknesses of his temperament, then you have an opportunity to help him become strong in those areas. If it is not a weakness in his temperament, then what has happened to make him respond in such a way? How can you help him overcome any insecurity that has taken control of his thinking? How can you give him opportunities to feel better about himself, to have improved self-worth? Does he have an above-average natural ability that you can help nurture and develop?

You have a great opportunity to refine and improve your child's strengths and weaknesses that are part of his unique temperament traits. As you spend time studying your child and familiarizing yourself to these four temperaments, you will find increased passion and purpose in developing your child's character.

Taking time to understand your children's temperament will reap great relationship rewards. You will love them better. You will parent them better. You will enable them to love others better. You will thoroughly enjoy, adore, and cherish the unique personality they possess.

Our Distinguishing Personality
(Supplementary questions for personal or group discussion)

1. If you have access to the Internet, search out free online tests to find out what your temperaments are. Share what you find out about yourself.
   - What areas of weakness are listed for your temperament that would be good for you to improve on? Why?
   - What are four of the best qualities of your temperament that have helped you become a great parent? (If you cannot answer this, ask someone to point them out to you.)
2. List the two most dominant temperaments that you think your child has.
   - List the strengths of your child's temperaments that you think are a blessing and benefit to your family.
   - What areas of weakness are within your child's temperaments, and how can you encourage growth and help nurture those areas?
3. How has learning about your child's temperament helped you so far in parenting him/her differently?

Part Four
The Way We Maintain Peace:

Responding and Resolving Conflict
The Route to Obedience: Discipline
The Way We Enjoy Parenting

9
Responding to and Resolving Conflict

Do nothing from selfishness or empty conceit, but with humility of mind let each of you regard one another as more important than himself; do not merely look out for your own personal interests, but also for the interest of others.
Philippians 2:3–4
(NAS)

No matter how calmly you try to referee, parenting will eventually produce bizarre behavior, and I'm not talking about the kids.
—Bill Cosby

I think the ultimate way to avoid all conflict is to not want or desire anything—to be so easygoing in life that nothing seems to upset or disturb your ecosystem of thoughts. Well, because this is not at all possible, even with the most positive and upbeat personality, I think it is best to deal with what comes first into our mind when a conflict arises: our expectations and desires.

All relationships have conflicts interwoven in them, but if your goal is to avoid conflicts, then your success rate is going to be high. When I try to avoid conflict, I make a conscious effort in my thinking process, which affects my speaking process. If I take note of what

I expect or desire from a person, then I will take steps to avoid a potential conflict.

Getting to the Emotions of Conflicts

Where does this potential conflict come from? My own heart, my own desire, and my own expectation (James 4:1–3). It also may come from the other person's desire and expectation. What you decide to do with that desire and expectation will produce peace or conflict in your own mind, heart, and relationship.

In a parent/child relationship, there is one area where conflict can be a daily battleground: the issue of disobedience. You cannot avoid this type of conflict, but the key is to focus on how you respond to the conflict and what you think about the conflict or disobedience. If you become controlled by your irritation, frustration, anger, depression, or sadness, then you are setting yourself up for unresolved conflict. You might turn it into a negative punishment for your child or let it prickle you, as a thorn of constant irritation.

I say "if you become controlled," because you probably will feel one of those emotions when a conflict arises—but are you going to allow that emotion to direct your response? You might discipline your child out of anger, frustration, self-pity, or some type of hopelessness, but if you think about your expectations and desire (such as teaching your child to obey you and God), then you have an opportunity to respond in a positive and productive way, thus resolving the conflict externally and internally. Yes, that still includes disciplining your child for disobeying, but your goal has switched from the desire to punish her to the desire to train her. Disciplining is training, not punishing. Having this attitude will produce a strong sense of control in your mind. As you take the emotion out of the conflict, you are able to look at the situation from a perspective of reaching the goal. Your goal is to train your child. When you can rise above the frustrations of training your child, it will calm the conflict in your heart and help you focus on the goal ahead.

Lead by Example

Have you noticed how you respond to conflict? When there is a standoff or a strong disagreement with someone, what is your first response? Do you say something negative about the person's character or ability? Do you blame the person for the problem, deny any responsibility, or walk away without a word?

The best thing you can do when a conflict arises in a relationship is decide to either overlook (forgive) the remark or action, or talk to the person in a calm, polite, and loving way about your feelings and opinion. If the outcome is not resolved in the way you had hoped, you need to be ready to let it go and forgive. The next best thing you can do when a conflict arises is to acknowledge what you have done wrong, whether it was the words you chose or how you said them (tone, facial expressions, or body language), and then apologize.

As you parent your children, remember they are watching how you deal with and talk to others and how you resolve conflicts with your spouse, family members, and friends. They watch how humble and apologetic you are, how much you are willing to look at your own failures, and how eager you are to ask for forgiveness. Above all, they are affected by the way you choose to resolve and respond to conflict with them. Your goal is to teach your children to love and respect others. They need to learn to resolve conflicts with you and with their siblings, friends, and eventually, with their future spouse.

Your relationship with your spouse is most likely the one that is on display. Let's say you run errands one day, leaving your husband to watch the kids at home. When you return, you find out he allowed the kids to eat right before dinner. Not only that, but he did not discipline Carly for getting into the candy drawer and sneaking candy to her room. The kids are in the family room with your husband when you ask him why he let the children eat before dinner and why he didn't do anything about Carly's disobeying. He says that he didn't think about it being close to dinnertime, and he did tell Carly not to do it again as he took away the candy.

Now, it would be my nature (without submitting to the Holy Spirit's influence) to let my husband know exactly how he had failed as a parent—failing to manage the children's time wisely and allowing Carly to have no consequences when she disobeyed the rules. But the correct response would be to tell him (calmly and politely) why it is not good for the children to eat before dinner and that it is disappointing to spend time preparing dinner when the children aren't hungry enough to eat it. Then, I would ask him (again, calmly and graciously) if he could remember to check the time the next time the children ask for a snack. As for the lack of discipline, I would tell him, in the same tone, that I have been changing Carly's behavior by taking away her favorite doll every time she gets into the candy drawer, and that I would appreciate if he could keep an eye on that problem when I am not around.

If I'd responded the way I was tempted to respond at first, it would have insulted his abilities to care for the children. He would have responded negatively to my scolding—and the downward spiral would have begun. But even if I had blown it and responded negatively, I could have said I was sorry and moved in the direction of a peaceful and respectful conversation. Either way, I am giving my children an example of how to deal with someone who does or says something I do not like or approve of.

We want to apply effective conflict resolution and pass it down to our children. Our responsibility is not only to teach but also to lead by example. Bring conflicts out in the open, with clear and honest dialogue and with a purpose in mind to forgive, love, and show compassion toward one another.

Approach conflict by thinking in this way: how can this conflict produce a closer and more loving relationship, and how can I be the tool to promote it? Conflicts are opportunities to help the relationship move from an average relationship to one that is outstanding and long-lasting.

Responding to and Resolving Conflict
(Supplementary questions for personal or group discussion)

1. What expectation/desire do you have for your child that could be causing unnecessary conflict in your relationship?
2. What thought frequently comes to your mind when you become frustrated or angry when your child disobeys you?
3. What is your first response when someone strongly disagrees with you, or is not kind to you, or says something that is hurtful or disrespectful?
4. Look up the following verses in the Bible about forgiveness and explain which elements are involved in forgiving someone (Matthew 6:14–15, 18:23–35; Ephesians 4:31–32, Colossians 3:13, Mark 11:25, Luke 17:3–4).
5. Are there conflict issues going on in your marriage that could be showing your child the wrong way to handle conflicts? If so, what can you do this week to change that?

10
The Route to Obedience: Discipline

Train up a child in the way he should go, even when he is old he will not depart from it.
Proverbs 22:6
(NAS)

I've noticed that one thing about parents is that no matter what stage your child is in, the parents who have older children always tell you the next stage is worse.

—Dave Barry

It seems most people do not like to use the word discipline when referring to dealing with their children's behaviors. The word discipline has a negative, harsh, and undemocratic feel to it. The Greek word used for discipline in the New Testament is *paideia* (Ephesians 6:4; 2 Timothy 3:16; Hebrews 12:5, 7, 8, 11). *Paideia* means to train and educate a person in mind, body, and morals. It carries the idea of completely training that person's character and physical body. I would say that is exactly what we do when we discipline our children—we are training them to eventually think and act like an adult.

I like the etymology of the word discipline, which I found on Dictionary.com.[6] One of the origins of the word discipline is "instruction given to a disciple." Do you remember the goal of parenting mentioned in chapter two? Evangelism and discipleship. Remember the passage in Matthew 4:18–19 in which Jesus tells Peter and Andrew he wants to "make them fishers of men." Jesus's goal was to spend time with them, to train them in the ways of God, and to reproduce himself in them. It took a great deal of time to train and change their character.

I think we can put a positive spin on the word discipline if we think of it more as training our children to be persons of quality and character. Think about training your child to be more like Jesus. This training process will take on many different forms—disciplining your child can look different from child to child, from parent to parent. The point is, whatever form of discipline you choose, choose it only if it works for that particular child. What works for one may not work for another. But before we get into the different methods, let's look at the starting point of a possible discipline issue.

As you reevaluate your discipline strategy, you may want to look at your own desire in getting your child to obey you. Look back to chapter nine, where I talk about dealing with conflicts. Check yourself for your desires in what you are expecting from your child that do not reflect or accompany God's desires for your child. Evaluate if you are reacting in an ungodly fashion if you do not get that desire met. Ask yourself why you want this or that from your child. How does it make you feel when your child does not meet that expectation? Is this expectation for your child going to benefit only you? If it will benefit only you, chances are there is something not right about that desire or expectation.

What message are you giving your child when she does not meet that desire/expectation? Is it shame, disapproval, and rejection of him/her as a person? Make sure you have not put unreasonable, premature, selfish, unattainable standards of obedience on your child. It will not produce the character quality or the relationship you are longing for her to have and share with you.

Let me give you an example: Donna is a great mom. She loves her daughter and enjoys being a stay-at-home mom. Donna does not approve of spanking as a form of discipline, so she has found another method. When Donna's daughter does not obey her, Donna turns her body away from her daughter. She turns away to show her daughter she does not approve of her behavior. I am glad Donna has found a form of discipline that works for her, but Donna is creating additional behavior problems down the road for her daughter.

By using rejection as her form of discipline, Donna is breeding a sense of approval-seeking in her daughter. Donna may not realize this right now, but she is manipulating her daughter to obey by demonstrating a rejection of her when she disobeys. This discipline strategy creates a conditional love relationship. Donna needs to show her child she loves her no matter what she does but at the same time, Donna needs to show and tell her daughter that she does not approve of her actions.

It is good for a child to be disciplined in love without manipulating emotions. The law of consequence is one action that creates a reaction—not that the child's action will determine your love and acceptance of him as a person. Donna is not using a method of discipline that will produce a certain character quality in her daughter or a healthy, independent, long-term relationship with her daughter.

Let's get back to the different methods of discipline. You probably have used the time-out method, but do you use it long enough? For a five-year-old, time-out can be around five minutes.[7] It is a short time for us but an eternity for a five-year-old. Along the same lines, one minute is a long time for a one-year-old but could be adequate time for discipline.

I would guess you have tried most of the other methods of discipline: spanking, consequences, denying privileges, or distracting them. What is your choice of discipline? Is it spanking? If so, have you thought about how old your child should be before you begin to spank? I have heard you should not spank a child under the age of two.

I think we should apply discernment and wisdom when determining how old a child should be before certain discipline methods are applied. If your child does not completely understand that she is disobeying you when she is younger than two, then discipline would not produce obedience in her thought process. But if it is apparent that she indeed does understand what you told her, then you could reevaluate if spanking or other discipline methods would be effective.

It becomes a bit more difficult with older children; you might need to narrow the methods. Time-out, spanking, and distraction may not be an effective motivator in obedience with preteens and teenagers. I guess the upgrade of time-out would be to ground them. Hopefully, by the time your child is a preteen or teenager, you will have instituted conflict resolutions, and you will have been consistent in training them to respect your authority. If so, then you will need only the occasional grounding, consequences, removing privileges, or the good ol' theory of giving them extra chores.

In whatever method you choose to train them, make sure it is done through grace, love, and patience. You might want to reread those chapters in light of reading this chapter on discipline.

I believe all these methods of dealing with training and disciplining your child are valuable in the proper timing and with each unique child and circumstance. Consequences usually work best with children older than age one or two, while distraction works best with children a year old and under. It all depends on your child's ability to understand your command and his ability to follow through with it. Children individually develop, physically and mentally, at different rates. Depending on their personality, some children are emotionally crushed when you apply a certain discipline. It may be too harsh for their personality, but then another child, whose personality is different, might need a more stern discipline. It might be a mistake on the parents' part to expect too much too soon. Patience and understanding are crucial when it comes to training your child to obey.

The Root of Disobedience

If possible, get to the root of why your children are disobeying. What is the underlying reason for their attitude? Are they bored? Tired? Hungry? Are they jealous of your attention to someone else? A toddler may be frustrated by her physical limitations. Is she testing the limits you have placed on her—testing you to see if you really mean what you say? Or is she going through the rulebook of what not to touch or do by touching or mimicking what not to do?

With children above toddler age, you might want to sit down and have a meaningful, heartfelt conversation, asking why they are struggling to obey this or that rule. Begin by assuring them they are free to voice their opinions because you respect them, and you are willing to negotiate if it is not harmful or unhealthy in any way. But let them know you have preferences for the way you are raising the family, and some things are not on the negotiation table.

If you are a parent who has established a lot of restrictions, it would be wise to find ways to bless your child with other privileges and freedoms that fall outside of your restrictions. I think the guideline for putting restrictions and expectations on your child is Colossians 3:21, which says: "Do not exasperate your children, that they may not lose heart."

Children love structure and a schedule; they love to know what is going to happen today. Routines bring security to a child's emotions. If you live a chaotic life, running around everywhere with your kids, it can disturb them and cause insecurity, anxiety, fatigue, and unsettledness. A routine creates stability; it causes them to feel safe and secure because they have experienced the routine repeatedly, and they can depend on its happening. As adults, we like routines just as much as our children do. Why? Because it brings the same sense of security to our lives. If your children show signs of unsettledness or of being overly tired or overstimulated, maybe a change in your daily routine is in order. You can establish routines and responsibilities into their daily lives. Encourage them to help you plan the day or week with the routines, responsibilities, and fun in mind. This gives them a sense of control over their lives as well.

A Plan of Attack

As you are raising your family, it would be advantageous to sit down with your spouse and create a road map of your discipline strategies. Decide beforehand what the discipline is going to be when the children disobey. Have your own rules in place before disobedience happens. Be proactive—plan your discipline in advance.

What are you going to do every time your child throws food on the floor from her high chair? Are you going to train her that when she throws her food on the floor, mealtime is over? Will you train her that whatever falls on the floor, stays on the floor, never to be returned? Will you pay attention to her time frame of eating, watching for when she is finished so you can remove her from the high chair immediately and not return her to the high chair to continue eating?

What are you going to do when he does not pick up his toys when asked? Will you take away those particular toys for a few days? Will you spank, give him a time-out, or deny a privilege? It is a wise and profitable thing to create a discipline plan—a set course when there is opposition, an attitude, or a relational issue, instead of dealing with it in haphazard, last-minute decisions.

As you decide what your response will be and what the discipline will be beforehand, tell your children in advance what the discipline will be if they disobey. Also, before you discipline them, remind them what you will need to do or what they will need to do, such as: "If you do not stop throwing your toys, then you will have to put your toys away," or "I will put your toys away."

Train them to understand and believe you always will respond to their attitude and action, whether the action and attitude are positive or negative. Remember, we want to tell them we appreciate their good attitude or thank them for their good behavior, too.

Consistency is the key to success in the training process of obedience. Try to always make eye contact or at least make your children acknowledge your request when you give them a direction. Teach them by giving them a warning for the first few times, but after you make sure they know your expectations, you should always follow through with discipline the first time they choose to disobey. If you and your child are away from home when he disobeys, simply say, "When we get home, I will need to discipline you for not obeying."

Build up your children's character when they show you character qualities that are worthy. Children, no matter what their age, need to know you adore them and respect them, as well as understanding the specific reasons why you adore and respect them. It is never too early or never too late to show you hold them in esteem.

I still remember a trip to the grocery store when my children all were very young. I had my budget in mind and a calculator in hand. Now, the trick was to get through the store with all three following me closely and to experience peace in the checkout lane. But then I would hear the whining about their wanting what their little eyes saw on the checkout shelves (you know—where they keep all the candy and cute little toys that cost too much on a cheap budget).

I really got tired of dealing with the whining, so I warned them if they whined and asked for candy the next time we were at the store, they would not be allowed to go to the store with me the next time I went. I told them I would have to go to the store by myself when Daddy got home from work. I also reminded them before we went into the store about not whining or asking for candy and toys. But to my disappointment, they forgot what I had said or misplaced it somewhere in their brains. I had no choice but to follow through with my promise. The next time I went to the store, they all were left behind with Daddy. They loved being with Daddy, but they also realized they'd missed out on a field trip. After a few times of being left behind, I asked them if they were willing to obey the new rule. After a while of them showing obedience to the new rule, I worked it into my budget to give them each a quarter to buy a piece of candy when we did our weekly grocery shopping. I wanted to bless their obedience in some tangible way.

Matters of Discipline

A common question I get is "Should you discipline in a public place?" My answer usually is, if you are in a friend's or relative's home, treat your child with respect and love. Take him into a private part of the home, have a talk with him, and discipline, if needed. When you discipline your children in front of their friends or in front of other adults, it embarrasses your children. It can be a degrading and shameful experience for them. I believe you or I would feel the same way if someone scolded or harshly corrected us in front of others.

If you are in a public arena, I would follow through with the promise of discipline upon arriving home. I would also follow through with the promise, "If you disobey me in public, you will not be allowed to go with me the next time." Prepare them for obedience when you leave the house. Go over your expectations again, reminding them what the consequences are if they choose to disrespect you or disobey you.

I don't think it is a good rule to reward them for future good behavior, such as, "If you obey Mommy at the store, you will get a piece of candy." You really want to teach them to obey you, because this is the way they show you respect and love, just like we obey God because we love him and respect and revere him. You can bless your children and reward their obedience after they have learned to obey without being reminded or warned.

It is respectful and nice of you to tell them why they are being disciplined. This will give them the opportunity to recognize where they went wrong in their decision making. It will also give them an opportunity to disagree or discuss why they think they should not be disciplined. Parents make judgment mistakes too; we sometimes do not see or hear perfectly. Say something like this to your child: "Did I ask you to pick up your toys?' The child says, "Yes." "Did you pick up your toys?" The child says, "No." You say, "You disobeyed me, so now I need to discipline you. Next time I ask you to do something, will you obey me?" "Yes," the child says. After you discipline, say something like, "I love you. Let's ask God to help you obey next time."

Keep in mind the limitations of what your child can understand, learn, and obey, based on each child's development and age factor. As you give instructions, be more detailed than a quick two-word command like "Be good"—explain exactly what you want from him. Or when you ask him to pick up his toys, give him detailed instructions, such as, "Pick up the toys you have been playing with this morning and put them into the basket in your closet." You are training him what that phrase means by giving him the details of the command the first several times you ask him to pick up his toys.

Another question I get is "Do you think whining is disobedience?" Whining is quite irritating to a parent; it definitely is a strategic maneuver of the child to get what he wants. Whining is not showing respect; it is not coming under authority. It is a form of arguing or complaining. Philippians 2:14–15 says, *"Do all things without grumbling or questioning, that you may be blameless and innocent, children of God without blemish in the midst of a crooked and twisted generation, among whom you shine as lights in the world"* (ESV).

A child shows respect to his parent through obedience. Showing respect is really showing reverence toward your position in her life. It is a good idea to teach your child what respect looks like through the window of obedience. Teach your child how to respond to someone respectfully through words and actions. You can ask your child how he could have spoken or acted that would have shown respect, instead of the word or action he said or did that showed disrespect. This means that you need to show respect to him also in the way you speak and act toward him. You are his role model; your words need to be validated by your actions.

Remember to balance your time of discipline with the time of love and grace you give your children daily. Too much discipline, too much control will enhance and encourage disobedience and rebellion. Remember to give them some choices and freedom—not in everything but in some things. Remember to love them in and through the discipline.

Remember that your child wants to please you, so affirm him and try to say yes to more things. Pay attention to your child throughout the day, not just when he disobeys or runs a little wild. Focus on him when he does nice and pleasant things. Verbalize how proud you are of her or how much you love her because of this or that. Think about your relationship with God: you obey him because you love him, and you know he loves you. This love relationship causes you to want to please him in what you say and do in life. The same is true of your child; he wants to please you because he loves you, and he knows you love him.

In his heart he desires a loving, secure, peaceful relationship with you, but his own selfish desires get in the way of that deep desire in his heart. Just remember that the healthy, holy love relationship you build with him will increase his ability and desire to obey you.

The Route to Obedience: Discipline

(Supplementary questions for personal or group discussion)

1. What did discipline look like when your parents were raising you? Do you agree or disagree with the method of discipline they used?
   - How different are your discipline methods from your parents'?
2. According to the definition of *paideia*, describe how you train a person to learn something.
3. Can you think of a negative message you might be giving your child when she/he does not meet your expectations of obedience? How can you translate it into a productive and valuable message? (Refer back to paragraph five of this chapter.)
4. Can you think of any changes you would make in your discipline strategy? If so, what changes are you planning to make?
5. What is the goal of your discipline in parenting? Does it meet with God's goal?

11
The Way We Enjoy Parenting

Now may the God of hope fill you with all joy and peace in believing,
that you may abound in hope by the power of the Holy Spirit.
Romans 15:13
(NAS)

The trouble with being a parent is that by the time you are experienced,
you are unemployed.

—Unknown

I cannot tell you how many times I have heard comments from a mom or dad about their feelings on parenting that conveyed they "grin and bear it." I remember very clearly one day when I attended an estate sale. I came across something in the pile of treasures that I thought my then-teenage daughter would love, which I mentioned to the woman next to me. Her response really made a marker in my memory. She said, "Teenagers! I hate parenting teenagers. It has been the worst job I have ever had!"

I still remember the thought that rushed through my mind when I heard her words: "I am so glad I love being with my teenagers and have a relationship with them." I was sincerely sad for this woman. I knew she probably had validity in what she was proclaiming, because that was her experience in parenting.

The teenage years of parenting seem like going through boot camp at times. It is exhausting to our emotions, our patience, and our communication skills. However, just like boot camp, it becomes easier with time and practice. Obviously, that is why your first child tends to gets the worst part of your parenting! You know a little more about parenting by the time your second child comes onto the scene.

Time Well Spent

One last element of parenting that I believe is of the utmost importance is to enjoy one another by having fun together. Family fun is essential if you want to build on family connection and communication. It helps repair the fallout from conflicts, too. Having fun together breaks down barriers in the parent/child relationship. It helps balance the relationship. In order to have joy and sweetness in the relationship, you must have periods of fun and relaxation together, not just the authority and responsibility of the relationship.

Make plans in your weekly schedule for family fun time. Play some board games, cards, checkers, or chess. Go to the library, park, museum, or special events in your city. Take in plays, musicals, or concerts. Sit down as a family and decide beforehand what you would like to do together, and have the children help you plan and prepare.

Build on some traditions that the family enjoys by making new traditions. My grown children have found security in some of the traditions my husband and I began in our family. I tried quite a few different potential traditions; some were successful, and some went in the trash. Experiment and find the ones that naturally stick.

Enjoy the outdoors by going camping, bicycling, or hiking. Our children all loved the outdoors and have fond memories of going to the lake, motorcycling, boating, camping, and just goofing off outside.

Eat together as a family. Make mealtime a warm experience, with good food and good conversations. Ask each other thought-provoking questions about faith, family, or world events. Ask questions concerning their favorite memories, favorite movies, or favorite food. Just think of things to ask and talk about during mealtime. You can plan a quick devotion to read at dinnertime too. Family devotions and praying together are great ways to connect at a deeper level; just make sure you keep it short and meaningful. Children do not need lecturing or preaching; they just need a shepherd to direct them and pray with them. One of my fondest memories of dinnertime was our family praying together. We decided that we would incorporate our family prayer time into dinnertime because of time limitations during the school year. Eventually, family prayer time became a standard thing we did at dinner.

Cooking was not my favorite thing to do as a wife and mom, so I focused on learning culinary arts. It gave me more purpose in my cooking. I learned the cuisine of other countries and served them to my family. Occasionally, we would celebrate the food of a particular country for one whole month. I would get a cookbook from the library that described the culture and the traditional food of that country. This made cooking more artful and purposeful in my mind. It also gave the children the opportunity to expand their palates. We found a lot of pleasure and enjoyment in the conversations around the table, too. I tried to plan dinnertime when the family all would be home at the same time. In our busy culture, that is a management skill in itself.

Find arts-and-crafts classes for children in your area. I used to sign up our children for relatively inexpensive art classes that the city offered in one of the historic homes in our city. There are so many things to do together as a family that do not cost a lot of money. Seek ideas from friends, family, the newspaper, parenting magazines, and your local chamber of commerce. Put the activities on your calendar and make preparations to actually do them. Waiting until the last minute to prepare will more than likely detour you and make you change your mind about doing anything.

Spend time with your children in helping other people. Take them to places where they can contribute something, such as donating some of their belongings or bringing something special they made or bought for someone. Take them to visit elderly relatives and/or friends that are homebound. I had a friend who took random opportunities to help someone in need, and she would incorporate her children in the act, no matter if it was a person who had a flat tire on the road or a lady in the supermarket needing help returning a grocery cart. I learned the value in what I saw my friend teach her children—to have compassion and mercy for others. Teaching them to be others-centered will encourage great growth in their maturity.

It All Points to Relationships!

You are building a love relationship with your child, from the moment you give birth to the day you or your child say good-bye at the moment of death. As your child and you look back on this love relationship you have strived to build, what do you want to remember? Do you want to remember only the trials of all the training, responsibilities, disappointments, failures, and conflicts? Or do you want those realities to be outweighed by all the times you went the extra mile to work through those trials, so that what came out of them—and you—was growth, maturity, heartfelt conversations, victory over conflicts and disagreements, grace, forgiveness, joy, and most of all, unconditional and sacrificial love for each other.

Hopefully, the things I have shared with you in this book are truths that will bring joy and peace into your parent/child relationship. As you see parenting as a call from God, I hope you will look forward to the process of transformation through which God might be taking you. This transformation has the promise of enabling you to mold and shape your child's character. Accepting and understanding the depths of God's grace, love, and patience will be your fuel to finish this job he has assigned you.

We have focused on taking time to understand the uniqueness of your child and to learn to communicate with purpose. Let me encourage you to take time to continue learning more about these things. Parenting is a job that needs continued education; there are many wonderful Christian books out there to aid you. You can visit the library or borrow books from a friend. Starting a book club with other moms is a great way to work through some parenting issues, with the author as the mentor. I have a decent-sized library of books that have ministered to and mentored me from the time I became a Christian, and I am still collecting and reading books that deal with all aspects of life.

The goal of Christian parenting is to pass on the faith that dwells in you. As you live out your faith-filled life before your children, teaching and exhibiting that kind of life, they will remember the process through which you took them—the process that took them to a place where your faith finally became their faith.

We have an incredible role in the life of our children. As we navigate through these parenting years, we are setting the course by providing the direction. Eventually, we will launch them onto their own journey of life. God is our compass. He will guide us through this process until completion.

The Way We Enjoy Parenting
(Supplementary questions for personal or group discussion)

1. What things prevent you from enjoying your children today?
2. In what tangible ways can you improve the overall enjoyment level with your child?
3. What are three ways you can increase the family fun in your life this week?
4. What do you want your child to remember about you and the way you parented her/him?

Notes

1. www.merriam-webster.com/dictionary/love
2. www.merriamwebster.com/dictionary/forbearance (Webster's Ninth New Collegiate Dictionary, 1991).
3. http://www.merriam-webster.com/dictionary/patient
4. Edward K. Rowell, 1001 Quotes Illustrations & Humorous Stories. (Grand Rapids, Michigan: BakerBooks, 2005), 930.
5. Gary Chapman, PhD, The Five Love Languages: The Secret to Love That Lasts. (Northfield, 2010).
6. discipline. Online Etymology Dictionary. Retrieved September 13, 2011, http://dictionary.reference.com/browse/discipline.
7. Focus on the Family, http://www.focusonthefamily.com/parenting/effective_biblical_discipline/approaches (Dobson n.d.).